the Barack Obama Miscellany

HUNDREDS OF FASCINATING FACTS ABOUT AMERICA'S GREAT NEW PRESIDENT

MARK HANKS

JOHN BLAKE

the Barack Obama Miscellany

HUNDREDS OF FASCINATING FACTS ABOUT AMERICA'S GREAT NEW PRESIDENT

MARK HANKS

JOHN BLAKE

Published by John Blake Publishing Ltd,
3 Bramber Court, 2 Bramber Road,
London W14 9PB, England

www.johnblakepublishing.co.uk

First published in hardback in 2009

ISBN: 978-1-84454-816-3

British Library Cataloguing-in-Publication Data:

A catalogue record for this book is available from
the British Library.

Design by www.envydesign.co.uk

Printed in the UK by CPI William Clowes Beccles NR34 7TL

1 3 5 7 9 10 8 6 4 2

Papers used by John Blake Publishing are natural,
recyclable products made from wood grown in sustainable
forests. The manufacturing processes conform to the
environmental regulations of the country of origin.

Contents

'Don't tell me we can't change.

'Yes, we can. Yes, we can change. Yes, we can.

'Yes, we can heal this nation. Yes, we can seize our future. And as we leave this great state with a new wind at our backs and we take this journey across this great country, a country we love, with the message we carry from the plains of Iowa to the hills of New Hampshire, from the Nevada desert to the South Carolina coast, the same message we had when we were up and when we were down, that, out of many, we are one; that, while we breathe, we will hope.

'And where we are met with cynicism and doubt and fear and those who tell us that we can't, we will respond with that timeless creed that sums up the spirit of the American people in three simple words – yes, we can.'

Barack Obama, January 2008

Obama Trivia

❈ Favourite restaurant: Topolobampo in the River North section of Chicago, Illinois, serving Mexican and regional cuisine in a classy setting.

❈ Favourite TV shows: *MASH* and *The Wire*.

❈ Favourite drink: black forest berry iced tea.

❈ Favourite suits: Hart Schaffner Marx costing $1,500 each.

❈ Obama wears a Secret Service watch (made in China).

❈ He gets a haircut every nine days at Zariff in Chicago at $21 per cut.

❈ He has four identical pairs of black shoes, size 11.

❈ Favourite children's book: *Where the Wild Things Are*.

❈ *Casablanca* and *One Flew Over The Cuckoo's Nest* are two of his favourite films.

❈ Obama loves to cook, and does a 'mean chilli'.

❈ The President collects comic books: *Spider-Man* is his favourite.

✹ As a teenager, he worked at Baskin-Robbins and these days he can't stand ice cream.

✹ He doesn't drink coffee or alcohol.

✹ Favourite musicians include: Bob Dylan, Miles Davis, Bach and the Fugees.

✹ Barack is said to be a superb Scrabble player.

✹ He is left-handed.

✹ On his desk he keeps a carving of a wooden hand holding an egg, which in Kenya is a symbol of life's fragility.

Favourite Books and Writers
Ralph Waldo Emerson, Thomas Jefferson, Mark Twain, Abraham Lincoln, James Baldwin, W.E.B. DuBois's *Souls of Black Folk*, Martin Luther King's *Letter From Birmingham Jail*, Toni Morrison's *Song of Solomon*, Graham Greene's *The Power and the Glory* and *The Quiet American*, Doris Lessing's *The Golden Notebook*, Alexandr Solzhenitsyn's *Cancer Ward*, John Steinbeck's *In Dubious Battle*, Robert Caro's *Power Broker*, Studs Terkel's *Working*, Adam Smith's *Wealth of Nations* and *Theory of Moral Sentiments*, and also Robert Penn Warren's *All the King's Men*. Friedrich Nietzsche, Reinhold Niebuhr and Paul Tillich.

* Barack's secret service codename is 'Renegade'.

* Obama carries a bracelet belonging to Sgt. Ryan David Jopek of Wisconsin, a soldier who was killed in Iraq.

* His favourite dish is Michelle's shrimp linguini.

* While at Harvard, Barack was rejected by an all-female committee after trying out for a pin-up calendar.

* He spent his first night in New York sleeping in an alley.

* Barack is 6' 1?" (1.87m) tall.

* His star sign is Leo.

* He read the entire Harry Potter series to his daughter Malia.

* He can bench-press 200 pounds.

* His desk in his Senate office once belonged to Robert Kennedy.

* Had he not been a politician, Barack would have liked to have been an architect.

✹ Barack means 'blessed' in Arabic.

✹ He hates the youth trend for trousers that sag beneath the backside.

✹ The Germans have paid tribute to President Barack Obama by rolling out some frozen chicken fingers bearing his name. A German frozen-food company has introduced Obama fingers. The tender, fried chicken bits come with 'a tasty curry sauce'. But Spiegel Online reports the company, Sprehe, 'was unaware of the possible racist overtones of the product'.

✹ Of the billions of searches carried out on the portal Yahoo.com over 2008, Obama was third behind Britney Spears and World Wrestling Entertainment.

✹ A 'shy' photographer in Indonesia is in great demand because of his resemblance to Obama. Ilham Anas, 34, is already a celebrity in Jakarta, where the President once lived, but his fame is spreading. He has appeared on Indonesia's premier TV talk show, appeared in an advertisement as Obama, and received other marketing offers from companies in the region.

✹ Barack is on Facebook.com, and has over 5.5 million friends (called supporters) who like to log on and poke the President. Martin Luther King provides Barack with his favourite quote: 'The Arc of the moral universe is long, but it bends towards justice.' Barack's wall contains nearly 600,000 posts, and Barack has posted nearly 2000 notes.

* His house in Chicago has four fireplaces.

* According to Obama, his worst habit is constantly checking his BlackBerry.

* He uses an Apple Mac laptop.

* He drives a Ford Escape Hybrid, having ditched his gas-guzzling Chrysler 300.

* During the presidential campaign, a huge range of merchandise became available – from Obama dolls, key rings, licence plates, earrings, stamps, wristbands to Obama wine, the list was endless. You could even buy Obama condoms – the packet bore the slogan 'Hope is no Protection'. Funnier still, Obama nappies were available. They carried a picture of Obama and the words 'Change we need'.

* Around the world, 1.5 billion watched America's first black President give his inaugural address.

* Logistics for the swearing-in ceremony were difficult for the inaugural planners. Jumbotron

TVs and 5,000 portable toilets were set up throughout the National Mall to accommodate the massive crowd. The number of toilets, as determined by the National Park Service, allowed one toilet for approximately every 300 people.

❋ While a record number of people attended Obama's inauguration, the overall cost was approximately $160 million. President Bush's inauguration, by contrast, cost approximately $42 million and was attended by 400,000 people.

Gamblin' Man

Barack loves playing poker. When he was a young state politician in Illinois, he used to attend weekly games at the home of Senator Terry Links, who has acknowledged that Barack played his cards right: 'He had the stone face. He didn't stay in hands if he didn't think he had a chance of winning. Barack wasn't one of those foolish gamblers who just thought all of a sudden that card in the middle was going to show up mysteriously. He's as competitive in politics as he is in poker.'

Denny Jacobs, a former State Senator who also played poker with Mr Obama, said, 'You find out a lot of things about a guy from the way he plays cards. Number one, Barack's conservative with his money, which is always good. It's hard to tell when he's bluffing. In fact, I never could – that's why he usually beat me.'

2

Early Obama

CHILDHOOD

❋ Barack Hussein Obama was born at the Kapiolani Medical Centre for Women and Children on 4 August 1961 in Honolulu, Hawaii, and he has the same birthday as Louis Armstrong and the Queen Mother.

❋ According to his birth certificate, Barack was born at 7.24pm.

❋ His father chose the Muslim name 'Hussein' in honour of Barack's grandfather Hussein Onyango Obama.

❋ Barack Obama Sr (the President's dad) was born in 1936 in the village of Kanyadhiang on the shores of Lake Victoria, Kenya, when it was a colony of the British Empire. He grew up herding goats and went to school in a tin-roof shack.

❋ At the age of 20, Obama Sr married a 16-year-old girl called Kezia in a tribal ceremony. He met her while on holiday in her hometown, and sent Kezia's parents 14 cows for her dowry. They set up home in Nairobi, where he was by this time working as a clerk.

At the age of 23, Obama Sr left for Hawaii on an economics scholarship, leaving behind his pregnant wife, Kezia, and one-year-old son,

Abongo, in the care of his father's third wife
Sarah Hussein Onyango.

✳ Barack's white American mother – Stanley Ann
Dunham – was born in 1942 at Fort Leavenworth,
Kansas, USA, while her father was serving in
the US Army. She was named 'Stanley' after her
father, because he wanted a boy and she was an
only child.

✳ Barack Sr and Stanley Ann met in 1960 while
attending a Russian class at the University of
Hawaii at Manoa – he was 24 and she was 18.
Obama Sr declared Ann a 'good woman' because
she waited for him when he was late for their
first date. Lucky for him (and us, if you think
about it), they married on 2 February 1961 in
Maui. No one was invited to the wedding.

✳ Barack's mother was already three months
pregnant when she married and was under the
impression that her new husband was a divorcee.
Mixed-race marriages were rare at the time in
America. In his autobiography *Dreams of my
Father*, Obama wrote that his father was as 'black
as pitch', while his mother was as 'white as milk'.

✳ Obama's father was the University of Hawaii's
first African student. He was the President of the
International Student Association at a time when

black people made up less than 1 per cent of
Hawaii's population. In 1963, Obama Sr left to
pursue a PhD programme in economics at
Harvard in Boston, despite a lucrative offer from
New York University that would have supported
the whole family.

※ Barack's mother filed for divorce in Honolulu in
January 1964, citing 'grievous mental suffering'.
Obama Sr did not contest the divorce. He went
on to attain his master's degree in economics in
1965 and was known as 'Mr Double Double' at
Harvard because of his penchant for double
Scotch. While studying, Obama Sr met Ruth
Nidesand who became his third wife. Ruth went
back to Kenya with him in 1965, where he
worked as a government economist in the Kenyan
Ministry of Economic Planning and Development.

※ Obama's mother went back to college, collected
Food Stamps and relied heavily on her parents to
look after Barack before marrying Lolo Soetoro,
an Indonesian master's graduate she had met at
the University of Hawaii. In 1967, she graduated
with a bachelor's degree.

※ Obama's stepfather Lolo had to return to
Indonesia when the government called home all
its citizens studying abroad. Mother and son
followed Lolo when Obama was only six years old.

☀ Jakarta was their new home. The city was lit by kerosene lamps at the time and they had no electricity in the house.

☀ During his time in Indonesia, Barack came face-to-face with real poverty and recalled a leper coming to their door one day with a hole where his nose should have been. He remembers it made a discomforting 'whistling sound' as he asked for food.

☀ Baby crocodiles, chickens and birds of paradise roamed freely in the family's backyard, and Obama played in rice paddies and rode water buffalo.

★ ★ ★ ★ ★ ★ ★ ★ ★ ★ ★ ★ ★ ★ ★

While in Indonesia, Obama kept a pet ape called Tata. He ate chilli peppers and sampled dog meat, snake meat and roasted grasshopper.

★ ★ ★ ★ ★ ★ ★ ★ ★ ★ ★ ★ ★ ★ ★

☀ It was in Jakarta that Obama attended the Roman Catholic Franciscus Assisi Primary School before moving to a school closer to the family's new residence.

☀ Obama's mother taught English to local businessmen at the US Embassy in Jakarta while Lolo worked as a government relations consultant with Mobil

Oil. Stanley Ann became more fascinated by Indonesia while Lolo became increasingly attracted to all things western. In 1969, Lolo was promoted and they moved to a better neighbourhood.

✸ The future President's daily routine was admirable. His mother woke him every morning at 4am to give him English lessons before school, as Barack's classes were taught in Indonesian. As a result Obama speaks Bahasa, the language spoken in Indonesia and Malaysia.

✸ The Indonesian ambassador to the US once said, 'Back home people think of him as one of us, or at least one who understands us.'

✸ Obama's mother encouraged him to read African-American literature and to listen to African-American music.

✸ Nicknamed 'Barry' and 'Curly Eyelashes' by his classmates, Obama was sometimes teased for having the initials B.O. His stepfather taught him to punch above his weight, after the little fella was bullied by an older boy at school.

★ ★ ★ ★ ★ ★ ★ ★ ★ ★ ★ ★ ★ ★ ★

In a school essay Barack claimed he wanted to be President when he grew up!

★ ★ ★ ★ ★ ★ ★ ★ ★ ★ ★ ★ ★ ★ ★

* Barack's half-sister Maya Soetoro-Ng was born in Jakarta in 1970 and named after Maya Angelou. Maya is a teacher and professor in Honolulu.

* Barack's mother sent him back to Hawaii at the age of ten to complete his education.

* Obama lived with his maternal grandparents Madelyn 'Toot' and Stanley Dunham in their two-bedroom apartment in Hawaii. They had been moved there through the Federal Housing Program after the Second World War.

* Stanley was a furniture salesman and an unsuccessful insurance agent, and Toot was the vice-president of a bank.

* In 1971, aged ten, Barack won a scholarship to Punahou School. Punahou is Hawaii's top prep academy, where the curriculum centred on multiculturalism.

* Barack's real father came to visit him once, at his grandparents' in Hawaii: 'Well, Barry, it is a good thing to see you after so long. Very good,' he said.
  Barack Sr delivered a speech before his class. 'Your dad is pretty cool,' one of Barack Jr's classmates remarked, but the young boy's father left after a month, never to be seen again.

★ ★ ★ ★ ★ ★ ★ ★ ★ ★ ★ ★ ★ ★

The young Barack didn't want to be seen as different from the other kids, but he couldn't resist pretending that his father was a prince, his grandfather a chief, and that his family name meant 'burning spear'.

★ ★ ★ ★ ★ ★ ★ ★ ★ ★ ★ ★ ★ ★

✺ Obama's mum and sister joined him in Hawaii in 1972, leaving Lolo behind.

✺ His mother enrolled in a master's programme at the University of Hawaii to study the anthropology of Indonesia.

✺ Obama was often seen carrying books in one hand (he was particularly drawn to the writings of Malcolm X) and dribbling a basketball in the other.

✺ Obama composed poetry for the school's literary magazine. In an edition called 'An Old Man', he wrote, 'He pulls out forgotten dignity from under his flaking coat, and walks a straight line along the crooked world.'

✺ Barack was one of three black students at Punahou School, which is where he first became aware of racism and what it meant to be an African-American.

* The Punahou basketball coach once upbraided the team for losing to 'a bunch of niggers'.

⭐ ⭐ ⭐ ⭐ ⭐ ⭐ ⭐ ⭐ ⭐ ⭐ ⭐ ⭐ ⭐ ⭐

As a teenager, Obama used alcohol, marijuana and cocaine to 'push questions of who I was out of my mind'.

⭐ ⭐ ⭐ ⭐ ⭐ ⭐ ⭐ ⭐ ⭐ ⭐ ⭐ ⭐ ⭐ ⭐

* Obama once wrote, 'The opportunity that Hawaii offered – to experience a variety of cultures in a climate of mutual respect – became an integral part of my world view, and a basis for the values that I hold most dear.'

* Obama's mother returned to Indonesia in 1975, when Barack was just 14, to do anthropological fieldwork for her PhD.

* Obama graduated from high school in 1979.

UNIVERSITY AND EARLY CAREER

* Obama won a scholarship to attend Occidental College in Los Angeles, one of the oldest liberal arts colleges on the West Coast. He had been accepted into several good colleges, but chose Occidental mainly because he'd met a girl from Brentwood while she was vacationing in Hawaii.

* Obama helped the JV Tigers basketball team at Occidental to an undefeated season.

❋ Barack also gave a brief but well-received speech to kick off an anti-apartheid demonstration.

❋ Joking about a Mexican cleaning woman's distress at the mess he and his friends had left after a party, Obama was jolted back to reality by a fellow black student: 'You think that's funny?' she asked. 'That could have been my grandmother, you know. She had to clean up after people for most of her life.'

❋ At the end of his sophomore year, Obama transferred to Columbia University in New York. He majored in political science, specialising in international relations.

❋ He told his relatives he wanted to be called Barack and not Barry.

❋ While at Columbia, Barack became involved with the Black Student Organization and anti-apartheid activities.

❋ Barack's mother filed for divorce from Lolo in 1980.

❋ Barack's father remained sporadically in touch. He was in several alcohol-related car accidents in Kenya, one of which resulted in the loss of both legs, and he died in a car crash in Nairobi in 1982 at just 46 years old.

❋ Barack's mother went to Kenya after Obama Sr died. She met his first wife, Kezia, and they became the best of friends. Stanley Ann also received her master's degree from the University of Hawaii in 1983.

★ ★ ★ ★ ★ ★ ★ ★ ★ ★ ★ ★ ★ ★ ★

Barack graduated from Columbia in 1983, with a double major in English literature and political science, and a determination to 'organise black folks. At the grass roots.'

★ ★ ★ ★ ★ ★ ★ ★ ★ ★ ★ ★ ★ ★ ★

❋ His first job out of college was as a financial writer at Business International, a research service in New York.

❋ Obama joined a public interest group in New York, campaigning for upgrades to the city's subway system.

❋ In 1985, Chicago elected its first black Mayor, Harold Washington. Inspired by this, Obama moved there at the age of 24. He became director of the Developing Communities Project (DCP), a church-based community organisation on Chicago's far South Side. Between 1985 and 1988, the staff at DCP grew from one to thirteen and its annual budget grew from $70,000 to $400,000. Obama helped establish a job training programme, a tutoring programme for would-be

college students and a tenants' rights organisation, while he was also working as a consultant and instructor for the Gamaliel Foundation, a community organising institute.

★ ★ ★ ★ ★ ★ ★ ★ ★ ★ ★ ★ ★ ★ ★

Obama was baptised at the Trinity United Church of Christ in 1988, and toyed with becoming a preacher, a journalist or a novelist. Eventually, he decided to pursue a career in law and he gained a place at Harvard Law School in 1988.

★ ★ ★ ★ ★ ★ ★ ★ ★ ★ ★ ★ ★ ★ ★

✴ Obama travelled to Kenya before starting at Harvard. He visited his relatives in the Nyanza province, and cried as he sat between the graves of his father and grandfather. Barack realised the struggles his father had faced, and it gave him a sense that the work he was doing, and would go on to do, was directly connected to his Kenyan family and their struggles.

✴ He funded himself through Harvard using student loans and by working. One summer, Barack worked for Sidley Austin, an elite Chicago legal firm where he met his future wife Michelle, an attorney at the firm who was assigned as his adviser.

★ ★ ★ ★ ★ ★ ★ ★ ★ ★ ★ ★ ★ ★ ★

**At 28 years old, Obama was elected president of
The Harvard Law Review, making him the first black
president in the legal journal's 104-year history.**

★ ★ ★ ★ ★ ★ ★ ★ ★ ★ ★ ★ ★ ★ ★

* Barack had to persuade Michelle for a month before she went on a date with him.

* On their first date, Michelle and Obama went to the Art Institute, strolled down Michigan Avenue and caught Spike Lee's movie *Do the Right Thing*. 'It was fantastic,' Michelle said. 'He was definitely putting on the charm … It worked. He swept me off my feet.'

* We clicked right away … by the end of that date it was over … I was sold,' Michelle said.

* Barack graduated from Harvard with a distinction.

* The young Barack's success at Harvard led to his first book deal, the poignant memoir *Dreams from My Father: A Story of Race and Inheritance*.

* Obama was offered lucrative corporate contracts, but turned them down to practise civil-rights law back in Chicago. He represented victims of housing and employment discrimination and worked on voting-rights legislation.

★ ★ ★ ★ ★ ★ ★ ★ ★ ★ ★ ★ ★ ★

Barack and Michelle married on 10 October 1992. Stevie Wonder's 'You and I' was their wedding song. Obama noted, 'I think it's fair to say that, had I not been a Stevie Wonder fan, Michelle might not have dated me. We might not have married. The fact that we agreed on Stevie was part of the essence of our courtship.'

★ ★ ★ ★ ★ ★ ★ ★ ★ ★ ★ ★ ★ ★

❋ Barack was an associate at Davis, Miner, Barnhill & Galland law firm from 1993 to 1996, then of counsel from 1996 to 2004. He also taught constitutional law at the University of Chicago Law School.

❋ In 1992, Obama was one of the founding directors of Public Allies – an organisation which advances new leadership to strengthen communities, non-profits and civic participation. He resigned before his wife, Michelle, became the founding executive director of Public Allies Chicago in early 1993.

❋ At the age of 31, Obama was named in the 1993 annual '40 under 40' list published by Crain's Chicago Business recognising the city's young leaders, stating he had 'galvanised Chicago's political community, as no seasoned politico had before'.

❋ Obama was brought into close contact with the city's Democratic political elite when Michelle worked for Chicago's powerful Mayor Richard M. Daley.

❋ From 1994 to 2002, Obama sat on the boards of two foundations who backed social and political reform – the Woods Fund and the Joyce Foundation.

❋ He was also president of the board of the Annenberg Challenge Grant, which distributed some $50 million in grants to public-school-reform efforts.

★ ★ ★ ★ ★ ★ ★ ★ ★ ★ ★ ★ ★ ★

During the 1992 presidential campaign, Barack directed Illinois's Project Vote, a voter-registration campaign which registered 150,000 of the state's 400,000 unregistered African-Americans. This led to Carol Moseley Braun becoming the first African-American woman to claim a seat in the Senate.

★ ★ ★ ★ ★ ★ ★ ★ ★ ★ ★ ★ ★ ★

❋ Obama served on the board of directors of the Chicago Lawyers' Committee for Civil Rights Under Law, the Center for Neighborhood Technology and the Lugenia Burns Hope Center.

✴ Obama was made Senior Lecturer at the University of Chicago Law School in 1996.

3

Political Obama

❋ On 19 September 1995, 34-year-old Barack Obama
announced his Democratic candidacy for the
Illinois State Senate seat to an audience of 200 at
the lakefront Ramada Inn in Chicago. The Illinois
Senate was controlled by Republicans at the time.
Springfield is home to the Illinois government.

★ ★ ★ ★ ★ ★ ★ ★ ★ ★ ★ ★ ★ ★ ★
**While Barack was running for the Illinois State Senate seat,
one veteran politician suggested Obama change his name,
while another told him to put a picture of his light-skinned
face on the campaign materials, 'so people don't see your
name and think you're some big dark guy'.**
★ ★ ★ ★ ★ ★ ★ ★ ★ ★ ★ ★ ★ ★ ★

❋ Obama's mother, Ann, died of metastatic uterine
cancer on 7 November 1995, aged 52. Barack
went to Hawaii to help his half-sister Maya scatter
their mother's ashes over the Pacific. Before she
died, Ann completed a 1,000-page thesis on
peasant blacksmithing in Indonesia and had been
working towards getting parts of it published.

★ ★ ★ ★ ★ ★ ★ ★ ★ ★ ★ ★ ★ ★ ★
**Obama has said his biggest mistake was not being
at his mother's side when she died.**
★ ★ ★ ★ ★ ★ ★ ★ ★ ★ ★ ★ ★ ★ ★

✺ *Dreams from My Father: A Story of Race and Inheritance* was published in 1995 to overwhelmingly positive reviews.

✺ In the March 1996 primary election, Obama won the Democratic nomination for State Senator for the 13th District of Illinois.

★ ★ ★ ★ ★ ★ ★ ★ ★ ★ ★ ★ ★ ★

On 5 November 1996, Obama was elected State Senator for the 13th District of Illinois, taking 82 per cent of the votes. That same year, President Bill Clinton became the first Democratic President to be awarded a second term in six decades.

★ ★ ★ ★ ★ ★ ★ ★ ★ ★ ★ ★ ★ ★

✺ Sworn in on 8 January 1997 for a two-year term as State Senator for the 13th District, Obama was made responsible for an area spanning Chicago's poorer South Side neighbourhoods – from Hyde Park-Kenwood through South Shore and from the lakefront west through Chicago Lawn.

✺ Obama lived in the Renaissance Inn on the edge of downtown Springfield while Michelle stayed back in Chicago. He played basketball at the YMCA in the morning and watched sports on TV, but always spoke to Michelle on the phone for an hour a night.

the Barack Obama Miscellany

✷ He took golf lessons and joined the senators' poker night, to which he brought a six-pack of beer. His fellow-players were all over 50 and white.

✷ Barack strongly wanted to lead black communities away from the unrealistic politics of assimilation, which he felt only helps a few people to 'move up, get rich, and move out'. He also opposed black nationalism because he believes it doesn't unify ordinary people or create realistic agendas for change.

★ ★ ★ ★ ★ ★ ★ ★ ★ ★ ★ ★ ★ ★ ★

Obama had an aide who advised him on how to be a 'regular guy'. Among the lessons were to order regular mustard, not Dijon, and not to wear button-down shirts.

★ ★ ★ ★ ★ ★ ★ ★ ★ ★ ★ ★ ★ ★ ★

✷ Obama started writing a regular column – 'Springfield Report' – for the *Hyde Park Herald* (his local Chicago newspaper) in February 1997.

✷ Obama quickly gained bipartisan support for legislation reforming ethics and healthcare laws.

✷ Some African-Americans resented this intellectual outsider. One favourite line was: 'You figure out whether you're white or black yet, Barack, or still searching?'

✺ Barack backed a law increasing tax credits for low-income workers, negotiated welfare reform and promoted increased subsidies for childcare before being re-elected to the Illinois Senate in 1998, defeating Republican Yesse Yehudah in the general election.

✺ In 1999, Congressman Bobby Rush – a former member of the Black Panther party – lost a challenge to Chicago Mayor Richard M. Daley. Obama saw this as his chance and decided to run for the Democratic candidacy for Congress.

✺ During the campaign, a pivotal vote on gun control legislation was due in the State Senate. When the vote came on the floor, Barack was in Hawaii visiting his 18-month-old daughter, Malia, who was ill. The gun control bill didn't pass and Barack came under fire for not attending the vote.

✺ Barack lost the Democratic primary run for the US House of Representatives to Bobby Rush by a margin of two to one. Following this, he experienced the 'not black enough' charge from several quarters for the first time in his political career. But there was a positive: while he may not have been a 'black' candidate, Barack realised that he was a blend of America, and that this could work in his favour.

Obama speaking on 11 September 2001: 'Even as I hope for some measure of peace and comfort to the bereaved families, I must also hope that we as a nation draw some measure of wisdom from this tragedy … We will have to make sure, despite our rage, that any US military action takes into account the lives of innocent civilians abroad. We will have to be unwavering in opposing bigotry or discrimination directed against neighbours and friends of Middle Eastern descent. Finally, we will have to devote far more attention to the monumental task of raising the hopes and prospects of embittered children across the globe – children not just in the Middle East, but also in Africa, Asia, Latin America, Eastern Europe and within our own shores.'

❋ Obama was one of the very few mainstream Democrats to oppose the Iraq war before it started. Addressing an anti-war rally in Chicago's Federal Plaza in October 2002, Obama denounced the planned invasion of Iraq, while repeating the line 'I don't oppose all wars.'

❋ The Democrats usurped Republican control of the Illinois Senate in 2002. That same year Obama was re-elected to the State Senate. In January 2003, Obama became chairman of the Illinois Senate's Health and Human Services Committee. He sponsored legislation to monitor racial profiling by requiring police to record the race of drivers they detained. He also sponsored legislation making Illinois the first state to authorise videotaping of homicide interrogations.

✷ Obama formally entered the race for the United States Senate in 2003. During the primaries, his Democratic rival, Blair Hull, took the lead, but after a short while dropped out when domestic-abuse allegations surfaced. Barack hired David Axelrod as his political strategist. Axelrod began filming Obama in public in 2003, footage he would later use to create a five-minute film for the internet for the 16 January 2007 announcement that Obama was running for President. 'Barack showed flashes of brilliance,' Axelrod said, 'but there were times of absolute pure drudgery... his speeches were very theoretical and intellectual and very long.'

★ ★ ★ ★ ★ ★ ★ ★ ★ ★ ★ ★ ★ ★

During his campaign for the Senate, Barack's aides thought he should have a driver but he refused: he liked having the time alone to clear his head.

★ ★ ★ ★ ★ ★ ★ ★ ★ ★ ★ ★ ★ ★

✷ In March 2004, Obama won the primary with 52 per cent of the vote.

✷ In the general election, Barack faced Republican candidate Jack Ryan, but Ryan was forced to

withdraw due to a sex scandal reported in the
Chicago Tribune. African-American Alan Keyes
replaced Jack Ryan, and soon questioned
Obama's Christianity and blackness.

★ ★ ★ ★ ★ ★ ★ ★ ★ ★ ★ ★ ★ ★ ★

**Obama's 2004 race against Republican Alan Keyes marked
the first time in US history that two African-Americans ran
as major party nominees for a Senate seat.**

★ ★ ★ ★ ★ ★ ★ ★ ★ ★ ★ ★ ★ ★ ★

✸ During the campaign, the police credited Obama
for his active engagement in enacting death-
penalty reforms.

> In August 2004, John Kerry asked Barack to be his keynote
> speaker at the Democratic National Convention address.
> 'There's not a liberal America and a conservative America,'
> said Obama in his speech. 'There's the United States of
> America. There's not a black America and a white America
> … there's the United States of America … We are one
> people …' The speech went out on primetime television to
> an estimated 9.1 million viewers. Barack Obama became
> famous overnight. 'Obamamania' was born.

✸ *Dreams from My Father* was reissued with a new
introduction by Obama and the DNC keynote
address. It became a huge bestseller. Nobel Laureate

Toni Morrison said Obama is 'a writer in my high esteem' and that his memoir is 'quite extraordinary'. The *Guardian* wrote that *Dreams from My Father* 'is easily the most honest, daring, and ambitious volume put out by a major US politician in the last 50 years', while the *New York Times* described it as 'the most evocative, lyrical and candid autobiography written by a future president'.

✹ In November 2004, Obama won the Senate seat, notching up 70 per cent of the vote. He was the fifth African-American Senator in the history of the US, and only the third to have been popularly elected. His step-grandmother, Kezia, attended his inauguration.

✹ The buzz about a presidential candidacy began before Obama had even been sworn into the Senate in January 2005. But Obama had told reporters in November 2004, 'I can unequivocally say I will not be running for national office in four years.'

✹ For the first nine months in Washington, Obama travelled nearly 40 times to the remotest corners of Illinois, holding surgeries in libraries and village halls. He worked 12-hour days and ate takeaway food at his desk. Every weekend he flew home economy class to see his wife and children in Chicago.

✻ Obama rented a one-bedroom apartment in Washington and began work on his second book, *The Audacity of Hope: Thoughts on Reclaiming the American Dream'*, aiming to set out his political vision.

★ ★ ★ ★ ★ ★ ★ ★ ★ ★ ★ ★ ★ ★

The Audacity of Hope: Thoughts on Reclaiming the American Dream was published in 2006 and shot to number one on both the New York Times and Amazon.com bestseller lists after Obama was endorsed by Oprah Winfrey. The book advance from the publisher totalled $1.9 million contracted for three books.

★ ★ ★ ★ ★ ★ ★ ★ ★ ★ ★ ★ ★ ★

✻ Obama's first law was passed with Republican Tom Coburn. The law allowed every American to go online and see exactly how tax dollars were being spent.

✻ He won a Best Spoken Word Grammy Award for the audiobook *Dreams of My Father* in 2006.

✻ According to the *Chicago Tribune*, the large crowds that gathered at *Audacity of Hope* book signings influenced Obama's decision to run for President. A former presidential candidate described the book as Obama's 'thesis submission' for the US presidency.

❋ The book remained on the *New York Times* bestseller list for 30 weeks.

❋ In December 2006, President Bush signed into law the Democratic Republic of the Congo Relief, Security, and Democracy Promotion Act, marking the first federal legislation to be enacted with Obama as its primary sponsor.

❋ Obama also introduced the Deceptive Practices and Voter Intimidation Prevention Act, a bill to criminalise deceptive practices in federal elections and the Iraq War De-Escalation Act of 2007, neither of which was signed into law.

❋ As a member of the Senate Foreign Relations Committee, Obama made official trips to Eastern Europe, the Middle East, Central Asia and Africa. He met with Mahmoud Abbas before he became President of the Palestinian Authority, and gave a speech at the University of Nairobi condemning corruption in the Kenyan government.

❋ Barack and his wife Michelle took HIV/Aids tests at Kisumu, which has one of Kenya's highest rates of HIV prevalence, encouraging local people to do the same.

❋ Thousands lined the streets of Kogelo at Obama's homecoming to his father's village.

✹ He visited the Senator Obama Kogelo Secondary School built on land donated by his paternal grandfather.

✹ On 10 February 2007, Barack Obama announced his candidacy for President of the United States in the 2008 US presidential election.

The Election Campaign

✳ Obama announced his intentions to run for President of the United States via a video on his website in January 2007. Then Senator for Illinois, he officially announced his candidacy for the presidency of the United States on 10 February 2007.

✳ A week before announcing his candidacy, Obama called for an end to negative campaigning: 'This can't be about who digs up more skeletons on who, who makes the fewest slip-ups on the campaign trail. We owe it to the American people to do more than that.'

✳ The announcement was made at the Old State Capitol building in Springfield, Illinois, where Abraham Lincoln delivered his famous 'House Divided' speech in 1858, which contained the immortal lines: 'A house divided against itself cannot stand. I believe this government cannot endure, permanently, half slave and half free.'

Barack had his own message: 'It was here, in Springfield, where North, South, East and West come together that I was reminded of the essential decency of the American people, where I came to believe that, through this decency, we can build a more hopeful America. And that is why, in the shadow of the Old State Capitol, where Lincoln once called on a divided house to stand together, where common hopes and

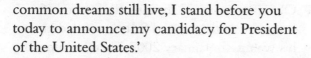

common dreams still live, I stand before you today to announce my candidacy for President of the United States.'

✳ The Chicago Mayor abandoned his tradition of staying neutral in Democratic primaries and endorsed Obama hours after his announcement. Former President Jimmy Carter stated his support for Obama. Meanwhile, after years of speculation, Democrat Hillary Clinton announced she was also running: 'I'm in, and I'm in to win.'

✳ Obama's campaign headquarters were at 233 North Michigan Avenue, Chicago, Illinois 60601.

✳ The Obama campaigners used a logo consisting of the letter O, with the centre suggesting a sun rising over fields in the colours of the American flag.

✳ Obama was the main challenger, along with John Edwards (former North Carolina Senator, making his second presidential bid), to Democratic Party frontrunner Hillary Clinton, who quickly established herself as favourite. She spent the first nine months of 2007 raising money and gathering endorsements while Barack lagged behind. By October 2007, Hillary Clinton was clinging to her 20-odd per cent poll lead.

Barack and the Media

- Barack's 'Yes We Can' speech set to music was viewed by 10 million people on YouTube in the first month, and received an Emmy Award.
- Time magazine named Barack Obama as its Person of the Year for his historic candidacy and election, which it described as 'the steady march of seemingly impossible accomplishments'.
- Eighty-eight per cent of the Obama campaign's donations came from online resources.
- Obama has a big presence on Facebook, MySpace, YouTube, Flickr and Twitter.
- The Washington Post gave Obama the title of 'King of Social Networking'.
- Obama spent a record-shattering $293 million on TV ads between 1 January 2007 and 29 October 2008. McCain spent just $132 million.
- The Obama camp lured Facebook co-founder Chris Hughes to build its own social networking site, myBarackObama.com.
- The website attracted more than 1.5 million members who organised themselves into 35,000 separate activists' groups, each of which could be contacted instantly from the Obama campaign headquarters to be given specific tasks in drumming up support.
- A total of 150,000 separate meetings and events were organised through the internet during the 21 months of Mr Obama's presidential campaign.

❈ Other Republican candidates in the running were: Fred Thompson, Senator turned *Law & Order* actor; Mitt Romney, Mormon and Governor of Massachusetts; former Baptist minister Mick Huckabee; and Rudy Giuliani, former Mayor of New York.

❈ The Obama campaign posted a question on Yahoo! Answers entitled: 'How can we engage more people in the democratic process?' which drew responses from over 17,000 people.

❈ By June 2008, Barack Obama had raised $349,716,137 for his presidential campaign run.

❈ Obama was criticised for being more aggressive than President Bush when he declared, 'If we have actionable intelligence about high-value terrorist targets and President Musharraf [of Pakistan] won't act, we will.' But later he stated, 'I never called for an invasion of Pakistan or Afghanistan,' and that, if reports showed Osama bin Laden in Pakistan, the US troops should enter only if 'the Pakistani government was unable or unwilling' to go after him.

❈ The Human Rights Campaign criticised Obama for bringing a Reverend McClurkin on the campaign tour, who claimed he was 'ex-gay' and that homosexuality was a 'curse [that runs against]

the intention of God'. The Obama campaign responded by adding a gay minister to the tour.

☀ Barack received over 500 death threats throughout the campaign, but played them down: 'It's not something that I'm spending time thinking about day to day. I think anybody who decides to run for President recognises that there are some risks involved.'

Campaign Number Crunch

2008 campaign price tag: $195 million in political ads Obama used the American flag in about 30 per cent of his adverts, while McCain's used the flag in over 60 per cent of his ads.

Obama used the word 'change' in about 39 per cent of his ads, while Clinton said it in only 10 per cent. In contrast, Obama used the word 'experience' in less than 2 per cent of his ads, while Clinton said it in 15 per cent of her ads.

☀ In October 2007, Obama began charging Hillary with failing to clearly state her political positions. A journalist in the *New York Times* wrote: 'Obama has appeared to struggle from the start of this campaign with how to marry what he has promised to be a new approach to politics – free of the partisan bitterness that has marked presidential campaigns for so long – with what it takes to actually win a presidential race.' That said, Obama began to climb again in the polls after a performance by Hillary Clinton at a Democratic debate in Philadelphia.

★ ★ ★ ★ ★ ★ ★ ★ ★ ★ ★ ★ ★ ★ ★

The United States Secret Service provided protection for Obama throughout the campaign, the earliest protection had ever been granted. Normally, presidential candidates are not offered Secret Service protection until early February of election year.

★ ★ ★ ★ ★ ★ ★ ★ ★ ★ ★ ★ ★ ★ ★

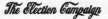 Obama's relationship to Bill Ayers, a former leader of a radical left organisation called the Weather Underground, was called into question by the media. Later investigations concluded that he and Obama didn't, in fact, have a close relationship.

★ ★ ★ ★ ★ ★ ★ ★ ★ ★ ★ ★ ★ ★ ★

When asked why he had stopped sporting a lapel pin of the American flag – which he had started wearing after the 9/11 attacks – Obama's response was that it had come to feel like 'a substitute for true patriotism'.

★ ★ ★ ★ ★ ★ ★ ★ ★ ★ ★ ★ ★ ★ ★

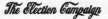 At a rally in November 2007, Hillary Clinton used phrases such as 'When I'm President'. But Obama's performance that same night overshadowed Clinton's and put him back in the running.

✳ Bill Clinton told voters that Obama's claim to have always opposed the war on Iraq was based on 'the biggest fairytale I've ever seen'.

★ ★ ★ ★ ★ ★ ★ ★ ★ ★ ★ ★ ★

Controversy arose over Obama's admissions of drug use as a teenager after he stated, 'Pot had helped, and booze. Maybe a little blow when you could afford it.' At a New Hampshire high school, Obama told students, 'I've made some bad decisions that I've actually written about,' noting that his 'drinking and experimenting with drugs' accounted for a lot of 'wasted time'.

★ ★ ★ ★ ★ ★ ★ ★ ★ ★ ★ ★ ★

✳ The turning point for Obama came in December 2007 when Oprah announced her support. She went on a campaign tour, drawing huge crowds in Iowa, New Hampshire and South Carolina. She was described as 'more cogent, more effective, more convincing' than anyone on the campaign trail. The Oprah–Obama tour dominated political news headlines.

★ ★ ★ ★ ★ ★ ★ ★ ★ ★ ★ ★ ★

Obama was the first major-party presidential candidate to turn down public financing since the system was created in the aftermath of Watergate.

★ ★ ★ ★ ★ ★ ★ ★ ★ ★ ★ ★ ★

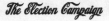

✺ Many candidates released Christmas videos. Obama chose one that gave speaking parts to his wife and daughters and emphasised a message of thanks and unity.

✺ By January 2008, Obama had a double-digit lead over Hillary in New Hampshire, and in February he sparked a row by saying American troops should be withdrawn from Iraq within 12 months.

✺ Clinton gave what sounded like a valedictory speech, praising Obama and saying 'whatever happens, we're going to be fine'.

★ ★ ★ ★ ★ ★ ★ ★ ★ ★ ★ ★ ★ ★ ★

For the first time in its history, Iowa put a black candidate at the top of the presidential election poll in January 2008.

★ ★ ★ ★ ★ ★ ★ ★ ★ ★ ★ ★ ★ ★ ★

✺ It was revealed that Hillary lent her campaign $5 million. Obama won the next 11 contests in February, pulling ahead in the delegate count. A Clinton supporter told a California newspaper that Obama wouldn't have been so successful if he had been white.

✺ In March 2008, Clinton won three of the four contests on the second 'super-Tuesday'. Super Tuesdays are the Tuesday in February or March of an election year when the greatest number of states hold primary elections to select delegates to national conventions where each party's presidential candidates are officially nominated. More delegates can be won on Super Tuesday than on any other single day of the primary calendar, and, accordingly, candidates seeking the presidency traditionally must do well on this day to secure their party's nomination. Hillary's wins put an end to calls among some Democrats for her withdrawal.

✹ It was revealed that Hillary Clinton was often absent during key moments of Bill Clinton's presidency, undermining her claim to foreign policy experience. Clinton – who criticised Obama as 'elitist and out of touch' – was forced to admit that she had exaggerated claims of coming under fire during a visit to Bosnia in the 1990s after video footage showed her walking calmly from her plane.

✹ One commentator declared, 'Obama is almost too cerebral for the sound-bite world of modern politics, but that's part of his appeal.'

★ ★ ★ ★ ★ ★ ★ ★ ★ ★ ★ ★ ★ ★ ★
'The Empire Strikes Barack', a video featuring Barack Obama as Luke Skywalker rallying from attacks by Hillary Clinton (portrayed as Darth Vader), was released online.
★ ★ ★ ★ ★ ★ ★ ★ ★ ★ ★ ★ ★ ★ ★

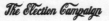

✸ In an effort to court gun owners, Hillary talked of learning to shoot as a child. Obama retorted with: 'She's talking like she's Annie Oakley.' Annie Oakley was a 19th-century American sharpshooter and exhibition shooter.

✸ Clinton threatened to 'totally obliterate' Iran if it launched a nuclear strike against Israel.

✸ Obama won North Carolina by 14 percentage points. Super delegates and influential Democrats streamed into Obama's camp, and before long he overtook Clinton's once substantial lead.

Obama Tube

- By August 2008, Obama had more than a thousand videos on YouTube and his MySpace page boasted 459,000 friends.
- A sexy music video called 'I Got a Crush … on Obama' appeared on YouTube in June 2007 and had over 15 million hits.
- will.i.am of Black Eyed Peas produced and recorded star-studded endorsement 'Yes We Can', featuring a long list of celebrity friends singing the words of Obama's impassioned New Hampshire speech, which was released on YouTube, generating millions of viewers.
- The video of Obama's speech 'A More Perfect Union' 'went viral' online, reaching over 1.3 million viewers on YouTube within a day of the speech's delivery.

✸ In May 2008, the 'American Politics' application on Facebook listed Obama as the 6–1 favourite over Hillary Clinton. By June 2008, Obama was estimated to have surpassed the 2,118 delegates needed for the Democratic nomination. Clinton refused to concede for several days, but, at a rally in Washington, DC on 7 June 2008, she finally admitted defeat, urging her supporters to back Obama and vowing to do everything she could to help him get elected.

✸ In July 2008, Obama travelled to Kuwait, Afghanistan, Iraq, Jordan, the West Bank, Israel, Germany, France and the United Kingdom, where he met Gordon Brown, Tony Blair and David Cameron.

✸ Jesse Jackson was caught on film disparaging Obama for 'talking down' to African-Americans and saying he wanted to 'cut [Obama's] nuts out'. He later apologised.

✸ On 27 August 2008, the Democratic Party nominated Obama to run for the office of the President of the United States of America. Barack was the first African-American in the history of American politics to be nominated by a major party.

✦ Three neo-Nazi skinheads were arrested for conspiring to assassinate Obama. The group planned to shoot Obama during his convention acceptance speech in Denver, which was to be delivered outdoors at a football stadium on 28 August 2008 – the anniversary of Martin Luther King's legendary 'I have a dream' address. Federal agents downplayed the plot as being of 'no credible threat' to Barack.

★ ★ ★ ★ ★ ★ ★ ★ ★ ★ ★ ★ ★ ★ ★

On a Fox News show, the affectionate fist bump shared by Barack and Michelle Obama was obliquely referred to as a 'terrorist fist jab'.

★ ★ ★ ★ ★ ★ ★ ★ ★ ★ ★ ★ ★ ★ ★

✦ Senator Joe Biden of Delaware was the Democrat Party's Vice Presidential nominee.

✦ Obama's Republican opponent was John McCain, a 71-year old Arizona senator and former naval pilot who spent nearly six years in a Vietnamese PoW camp.

★ ★ ★ ★ ★ ★ ★ ★ ★ ★ ★ ★ ★ ★ ★

Barack Obama and John McCain are nearly 25 years apart in age. This was the largest age disparity between two major party presidential candidates in history.

★ ★ ★ ★ ★ ★ ★ ★ ★ ★ ★ ★ ★ ★ ★

✹ McCain initially led in opinion polls after he
picked Alaska Governor Sarah Palin to be his
running mate, but his support slipped away as the
economy soured and concern about Palin's
qualifications grew. When asked which newspaper
she read, Sarah Palin replied, 'All of 'em, any of
'em that have been in front of me over all these
years.' And on Afghanistan she had this to say:
'They are also building schools for the Afghan
children so that there is hope and opportunity in
our neighbouring country of Afghanistan.'

★ ★ ★ ★ ★ ★ ★ ★ ★ ★ ★ ★ ★ ★

**The Republicans raised $1 million after Republican
Vice Presidential nominee Sarah Palin's acceptance
speech, while the Democrats raised $10 million in the
same 24-hour period.**

★ ★ ★ ★ ★ ★ ★ ★ ★ ★ ★ ★ ★ ★

✹ As news of the Wall Street meltdown broke,
McCain was telling voters, 'The fundamentals of
the economy are strong.'

✹ The liberal *New Yorker* magazine featured a cover
depicting Obama and Michelle as terrorists in the
Oval office. Obama was in Muslim gear, while
Michelle sported an Afro and an AK-47 slung
over her shoulder. The magazine's editor, David
Remnick, wanted the image to 'hold up a mirror'
to the absurd and often malicious rumours that

stuck to Obama's campaign. He also hoped his readers would be intelligent enough to get the joke.

✹ The Barack Obama presidential campaign set up a website, FightTheSmears.com, to debunk rumours about the senator.

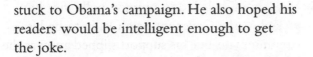

Pastor Disaster

Obama denounced his pastor Reverend Jeremiah Wright, whom he had known for over 20 years, after Wright asserted that the United States brought on the 9/11 attacks with its own terrorism and his assertion that 'the government lied about inventing the HIV virus as a means of genocide against people of colour'. Another 'pastor disaster' ensued when a video appeared on YouTube of a Catholic guest preacher at Wright's Trinity United church mocking Hillary Clinton's tears and accusing her of feeling she deserved to be President because she was white. Obama denounced Wright's remarks, but did not disown him as a person, and resigned his membership of the Trinity United Church of Christ.

✹ John McCain supported the war in Iraq while Barack Obama opposed it from the outset because there was no credible evidence that Iraq was tied to the attacks of September 11th.

❋ Obama proposed covering the healthcare of nearly 45 million uninsured Americans, reducing premium costs for everyone, and breaking 'the stranglehold' of the big drug and insurance companies. Domestic policy and the economy emerged as the main themes in the last few months of the election campaign after the onset of the economic crisis.

Obama's campaign announced a record fundraising total of $150 million for September 2008. Much of the Obama money came from a record-breaking number of small donations of $200 or less made online. Two Palestinian brothers bought T-shirts in bulk from the campaign's online store. They had listed their address as 'Ga.', which the campaign took to mean Georgia rather than Gaza. The campaign returned their $33,000. The Republican National Committee asked the Federal Election Commission to investigate the Obama campaign's screening practices.

❋ John McCain said in an interview that he was uncertain how many houses he and his wife, Cindy, owned: 'I think — I'll have my staff get to you.'

❋ A day before the election and a week after Barack Obama interrupted his campaign to visit her in Hawaii, the Democratic candidate's grandmother Madelyn Dunham died aged 86.

The Big Day

- Voter turnout on 4 November for the 2008 election was the highest in at least 40 years.
- It was the first election in 56 years in which neither an incumbent President nor Vice President had run.
- 131.2 million turned out to vote – that's 63 per cent of eligible voters – compared to 122.3 million in 2004. The African-American turnout increased from 11.1 per cent in 2004 to 13 per cent in 2008.
- Over 95 per cent of African-American voters voted for Barack Obama.
- Nine states changed allegiance from Republican in the 2004 election to Democrat in the 2008 election.
- On 4 November 2008, Obama won the presidential election, making him the 44th President of the United States, succeeding George W. Bush.
- Obama became the first African-American to win the White House.
- At 21 months, it had been the longest presidential campaign season in US history.
- Obama snared about 63 million (53 per cent) votes to McCain's 55.8 million.
- Obama received 365 electoral votes, and McCain 173.
- Barack received more votes than any presidential candidate in American history.
- McCain set the record for the most votes received by a losing presidential candidate with slightly less than 60 million votes.

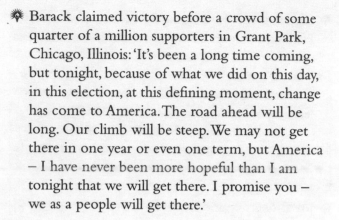

✹ Barack claimed victory before a crowd of some quarter of a million supporters in Grant Park, Chicago, Illinois: 'It's been a long time coming, but tonight, because of what we did on this day, in this election, at this defining moment, change has come to America. The road ahead will be long. Our climb will be steep. We may not get there in one year or even one term, but America – I have never been more hopeful than I am tonight that we will get there. I promise you – we as a people will get there.'

✹ He recited the words of Abraham Lincoln, the first Republican in the White House and the first President from Illinois: 'As Lincoln said to a nation far more divided than ours, "We are not enemies, but friends… though passion may have strained it must not break our bonds of affection."'

✹ Spontaneous street parties broke out in major cities across the United States, as well as in London, Bonn, Berlin, Japan, Toronto, Rio de Janeiro, Sydney, Nairobi and his father's village of Kogelo in Kenya.

✹ 'This is a special election. I recognise the great significance it must have for African-Americans and the special pride they must be feeling tonight,' said the defeated John McCain.

✵ Barack is the third sitting Senator, after Warren G. Harding and John F. Kennedy, to be elected President.

★ ★ ★ ★ ★ ★ ★ ★ ★ ★ ★ ★ ★ ★

Obama is the first President to be born outside the continental United States and the third President from Illinois, the first two being Abraham Lincoln and Ulysses S. Grant.

★ ★ ★ ★ ★ ★ ★ ★ ★ ★ ★ ★ ★ ★

✵ Joe Biden became the first Roman Catholic to be elected Vice President.

✵ On 20 January 2009, Obama was inaugurated to the presidency at the age of 47 years and 138 days. Tickets to the inauguration were being sold online for as much as $40,000 each. Entry should be free to anyone who requests and receives a ticket from his or her congressperson or senator.

Over two million people streamed into the Mall in Washington to see Obama being sworn in as the 44th President of the United States. The White House declared a precautionary state of emergency for the city because of the crowd. About 8,000 police were deployed and a total of 32,000 military personnel were either on duty or on standby. Large tracts of the city centre were fenced off and bridges over the river from Virginia were closed to traffic.

❊ The day before inauguration, Obama paid tribute to Martin Luther King: 'We will come together as one people on the same mall where Dr King's dream echoes still. My job in this speech and in my presidency is just to remind people of the road we've travelled and the extraordinary odds that we've already overcome.' As the first African-American President, he called himself 'an emblem' of that progress.

❊ Barack and Michelle attended a church service in the morning, then arrived at the White House for a cup of coffee with Mr and Mrs Bush and Vice-President Dick Cheney. Dick Cheney was in a wheelchair after pulling a back muscle.

❊ Obama arrived at Capitol Hill in an armoured limousine with George W. Bush.

❊ Barack appeared on the steps of the Capitol to vast cheers from the crowd and the chant 'Obama! Obama!'

❊ Aretha Franklin sang 'My Country 'Tis of Thee' just before Barack was sworn in. It was a cold day, and the singer wrapped her head in a crystal studded bow. The $179 hat, customised with Swarovski crystals, came from Mr. Song Millinery in Detroit where Luke Song has been making ladies' dress hats for 25 years.

★ ★ ★ ★ ★ ★ ★ ★ ★ ★ ★ ★ ★ ★ ★

**Mr Obama took the oath of office on a Bible used by his
hero Abraham Lincoln at his first inauguration in 1861.**

★ ★ ★ ★ ★ ★ ★ ★ ★ ★ ★ ★ ★ ★ ★

❋ Obama's swearing-in was followed by the US
Marine Corps band playing 'Hail to the Chief'
and a 21-gun salute.

❋ Senator Ted Kennedy collapsed during the
inaugural lunch and was rushed to hospital.

❋ There were days of celebration to follow, with
more than a thousand concerts, balls, dinners,
receptions and parties, ranging from the Creative
Coalition Gala Inaugural Ball, where tickets
started at $10,000 and rose to $100,000, to the
Black Cat club charging $10 to hear the 80s
punk band Anti Flag.

❋ George W. Bush left by helicopter bound for
Midland, Texas, before heading to the family
ranch at Crawford. He departed from office with
the lowest approval ratings of any US President.

❋ Among the celebrities celebrating were Tom Hanks,
Jamie Foxx, Denzel Washington, Beyoncé, Shakira,
Sting, Bono, Susan Sarandon, Bruce Springsteen,
the Beastie Boys, Jay-Z, Jack Johnson, Sheryl Crow,
James Taylor, Patti LaBelle and Harry Belafonte.

Inauguration Days

During the ceremony on the steps of the Capitol, Chief Justice John Roberts accidentally switched the word order when he administered the oath, saying, 'I will execute the office of President to the United States faithfully,' instead of, 'I will faithfully execute the office of President of the United States.' Obama, who briefly interrupted the Chief Justice by starting the oath before Roberts finished reciting the first part, then repeated back the line as Roberts had said it. Asked if he would be taking the oath again, Obama replied, 'I am. We're going to do it very slowly.' He took the oath of office again the following day, a Wednesday.

It's not the first time things have gone wrong at a presidential inauguration. Ronald Reagan's second inauguration in 1985 was cancelled because weather conditions were too dangerous.

Legend says that George Washington added the words 'so help me God' after taking the presidential oath. This has been disputed, but every President since 1933 has said them even though they're not required.

At John F. Kennedy's inauguration in 1961, the poet Robert Frost couldn't read a poem he had written specially for the occasion because of the sun's glare. He had to improvise by reciting a different poem that he knew by heart.

At Ulysses S. Grant's inauguration in 1873, a hundred canaries died as a result of 16-degree weather. Grant was reportedly unaware that small birds disliked below-freezing temperatures.

🦅 Oprah Winfrey was so convinced of Obama's victory she had bought her gown for the inaugural ball before election day.

🦅 There was a free open-air concert at the Lincoln Memorial headlined by Bruce Springsteen, Beyoncé, U2, Shakira, Usher, Stevie Wonder and Herbie Hancock, among others. This was followed by a 'Dreams of My Fathers' party at a swanky Washington hotel, featuring Alicia Keys, LL Cool J and Macy Gray.

🦅 Barack and Michelle had the first dance at the inaugural ball to Etta James's 'At Last' sung by Beyoncé.

🦅 The official partying ended when Barack and his family joined in a prayer service at the National Cathedral.

5

Obama's
First Lady

✸ Michelle LaVaughn Robinson Obama was born on 17 January 1964 on the South Side of Chicago.

✸ Her father, Fraser Robinson III, was a city water-plant employee and Democratic precinct captain.

✸ Her mother, Marian Shields Robinson, was a secretary at Spiegel's catalogue store.

★ ★ ★ ★ ★ ★ ★ ★ ★ ★ ★ ★ ★ ★

Michelle's great-great-grandfather, Jim Robinson, was an American slave in the state of South Carolina.

★ ★ ★ ★ ★ ★ ★ ★ ★ ★ ★ ★ ★ ★

✸ The First Lady is the first cousin, once removed, of Rabbi Capers C. Funnye Jr, one of the US's most prominent black rabbis.

✸ Michelle grew up in a one-bedroom apartment on Euclid Avenue in the South Shore community area of Chicago.

★ ★ ★ ★ ★ ★ ★ ★ ★ ★ ★ ★ ★ ★

Michelle and her brother, Craig (who is 21 months older), excelled at school and skipped the second grade.

★ ★ ★ ★ ★ ★ ★ ★ ★ ★ ★ ★ ★ ★

✸ Michelle admired her father and grandfather as 'bright, articulate, well-read men. If they'd been white, they would have been the heads of banks.'

✸ Her father, once a gifted athlete, was diagnosed with multiple sclerosis in his twenties. He never raised his voice to his children, but would fix them with a cold stare and say, 'I'm disappointed,' which used to make Michelle and her brother burst into tears.

✸ Michelle's brother Craig's basketball skills and brilliant grades won him a scholarship to Princeton. He is now the men's basketball coach at Oregon State University.

✸ Michelle steered clear of team sports at school because she couldn't stand the idea of losing.

✸ Michelle joined a gifted class at Bryn Mawr Elementary School (later renamed Bouchet Academy).

✸ She attended Whitney Young High School, where she was on the honour roll for four years, took advanced placement classes, was a member of the National Honor Society and served as student council treasurer.

✸ It took Michelle three hours to get to and from school each day. Santita Jackson, the daughter of Jesse Jackson, was a classmate.

✸ She majored in sociology and minored in

African–American studies at Princeton University, and spent her free time running a literacy programme for kids from the local neighbourhoods.

✷ Michelle wrote that Princeton 'made me far more aware of my "blackness" than ever before'. Her thesis was entitled 'Princeton-Educated Blacks and the Black Community'.

✷ 'I remember being shocked,' she said, 'by college students who drove BMWs. I didn't even know parents who drove BMWs.'

✷ She graduated from Princeton University in 1985 with a BA, and obtained her Juris Doctor (J.D.) degree from Harvard Law School in 1988. While at Harvard she took part in political demonstrations advocating the hiring of professors who were members of minorities.

★ ★ ★ ★ ★ ★ ★ ★ ★ ★ ★ ★ ★ ★
Michelle Obama is the third First Lady with a postgraduate degree, following Hillary Clinton and Laura Bush.
★ ★ ★ ★ ★ ★ ★ ★ ★ ★ ★ ★ ★ ★

✷ After graduating, Michelle worked as an associate dealing in copyright and trademark issues at the law firm Sidley Austin in Chicago, where she first met her husband Barack.

★ ★ ★ ★ ★ ★ ★ ★ ★ ★ ★ ★ ★ ★ ★

At first, Michelle dismissed Barack as 'a black guy who can talk straight', but he soon won her over when he took her to a community-organising session where he made a speech about closing the gap between 'the world as it is, and the world as it should be'.

★ ★ ★ ★ ★ ★ ★ ★ ★ ★ ★ ★ ★ ★ ★

※ Michelle said of their marriage: 'Barack didn't pledge riches, only a life that would be interesting. On that promise he's delivered.'

※ Her father passed away in 1991 of complications from MS. Around the same time, a close friend died of lymphoma. Considering her job at the time, Michelle said, 'If I died in four months, is this how I would have wanted to spend this time?'

※ Valerie Jarrett, deputy chief of staff, interviewed Michelle for a job at the Chicago Mayor Richard M. Daley's office: 'I offered her a job at the end of the interview – which was totally inappropriate since it was the Mayor's decision. She was so confident and committed and extremely open.'

※ In July 1991, Michelle went to work as Assistant to the Mayor, Richard M. Daley, and as Assistant Commissioner of Planning and Development.

✵ Michelle and Barack married in October 1992 in Chicago, Illinois.

✵ Michelle was Executive Director for the Chicago office of Public Allies for four years. This is a non-profit organisation that encourages young people to work on social issues in non-profit groups and government agencies. She set fundraising records for the organisation that still stood 12 years after she left.

✵ In 1996, Michelle served as the Associate Dean of Student Services at the University of Chicago, where she developed the University's Community Service Centre.

✵ After Barack's election to the US Senate, the Obama family continued to live on Chicago's South Side rather than moving to Washington, DC.

✵ Their daughter Malia Ann was born in 1998, and Natasha (better known as Sasha) was born in 2001.

✵ In 2002, Michelle began working for the University of Chicago Hospitals, first as executive director for community affairs and then as Vice President for Community and External Affairs. She inspired a programme to send doctors from the medical centre into community hospitals and clinics in poor surrounding neighbourhoods.

✳ Michelle's salary from the University of Chicago Hospitals was $273,618, while Barack's salary from the United States Senate was $157,082.

★ ★ ★ ★ ★ ★ ★ ★ ★ ★ ★ ★ ★ ★

When asked by her boss if there was anything about campaigning she enjoyed, Michelle said that visiting so many living rooms had given her some new ideas for decorating their house.

★ ★ ★ ★ ★ ★ ★ ★ ★ ★ ★ ★ ★ ★

✳ Michelle continued working during the primary campaign, but cut back to part-time in order to spend time with her daughters as well as work for her husband's election, subsequently taking a leave of absence from her job.

✳ Like any marriage, Barack and Michelle's relationship has had its ebbs and flows. The combination of family life and beginning a political career led to many arguments about balancing work and family. Barack wrote in his second book, *The Audacity of Hope: Thoughts on Reclaiming the American Dream*, that 'Tired and stressed, we had little time for conversation, much less romance'. But, despite their family obligations and careers, they continue to attempt to schedule date nights.

✺ Michelle was a board member of TreeHouse Foods, Inc., a major Wal-Mart supplier with whom she cut ties immediately after her husband made critical comments about them.

✺ Michelle helped campaign for her husband's presidential bid throughout 2007 and 2008, making a 'commitment to be away overnight only once a week, to campaign only two days a week and be home by the end of the second day' for their two children.

✺ In February 2008, Michelle attended 33 events in eight days.

✺ Michelle made at least two campaign appearances with Oprah Winfrey, and writes her own speeches and speaks without notes.

★ ★ ★ ★ ★ ★ ★ ★ ★ ★ ★ ★ ★ ★ ★

At a speech in Wisconsin, the woman introducing Michelle flubbed her line, saying she was 'honoured to introduce the next President'! Michelle joked that Barack was 'going to be the First Lady'.

★ ★ ★ ★ ★ ★ ★ ★ ★ ★ ★ ★ ★ ★ ★

✺ Asked in February 2008 whether she could see herself 'working to support' Hillary Clinton if she got the nomination, Michelle said, 'I'd have to think about that. I'd have to think about policies,

her approach, her tone.' She later added, 'You know, everyone in this party is going to work hard for whoever the nominee is.'

✳ When a reporter joked that Michelle could run for Barack's Senate seat if he were elected President, Michelle made a face of mock disgust. 'Ugh,' she grimaced. 'No, thank you.'

Quirky Michelle

• Within the family, her nickname is 'Miche' (pronounced 'Meesh').

• Barack calls her 'my Rock'.

• As a child, Michelle loved her Easy-Bake Oven.

• Even though she was only allowed one hour of television per night, she committed each episode of The Brady Bunch to memory.

• As a young girl, she practised playing the piano so much that she had to be told to stop.

• She hates wearing tights because it is 'too painful'.

• Michelle unwinds by watching reruns of The Dick Van Dyke Show.

• For breakfast, she likes fruit, eggs and bacon.

✳ Michelle has always insisted that Barack fly home from wherever he was to attend the girls' ballet recitals or parent–teacher meetings.

❋ When the couple hosted political gatherings at their home in Chicago, Michelle encouraged everyone to bring along their children.

❋ Michelle bought Barack and the kids laptops, so they could chat over the Internet.

❋ Barack made a deal with his wife: he would give up smoking in exchange for her support for his presidential campaign.

❋ Michelle liked to joke about Obama family life, but it wasn't always well received. One *New York Times* columnist wrote, 'I wince a bit when Michelle Obama chides her husband as a mere mortal – it's a comic routine that rests on the presumption that we see him as a god. But it may not be smart politics to mock him in a way that turns him from the glam JFK into the mundane Gerald Ford, toasting his own English muffin. If all Senator Obama is peddling is the Camelot mystique, why debunk this mystique?'

❋ In 2004, Michelle had said Hillary Clinton 'is smart and gracious and everything she appears to be in public – someone who's managed to raise what appears to be a solid, grounded child'.

❋ The First Lady employs an all-female staff of aides.

✸ Michelle was often labelled an 'angry black woman', to which she responded, 'Barack and I have been in the public eye for many years now, and we've developed a thick skin along the way. When you're out campaigning, there will always be criticism. I just take it in my stride and, at the end of the day, I know that it comes with the territory.'

✸ Michelle likes to tell the story of a little girl she met who told her that, if Barack won the White House, 'It means I can imagine anything for myself.'

✸ In February 2008, Michelle was criticised for saying, 'For the first time in my adult life, I am proud of my country because it feels like hope is finally making a comeback.'

✸ Michelle is three years older than Barack.

✸ Mrs Obama twice appeared on the *Vanity Fair* '10 of the World's Best Dressed People' list.

✸ *People* magazine also listed her as one of the best-dressed women in the US and praised her for her 'classic and confident' look.

✸ She was 58th on 'The Harvard 100' list in 2008, comprising the prior year's most influential Harvard alumni. Her husband was ranked fourth.

✸ Michelle wears clothes by designers Calvin Klein, Oscar de la Renta, Isabel Toledo, Narciso Rodriguez, Donna Ricco and Maria Pinto, and has become a fashion trendsetter.

✸ Michelle appeared on the cover of *American Vogue* in March 2009. According to the editor, Michelle chose her selections from her own wardrobe for the photo shoot. She had appeared on the cover once before, in 1998.

✸ Michelle installed a beehive at the White House. Charlie Brandts, a White House carpenter for 25 years, is now the First Beekeeper. He got the ball rolling when he told some of the East Wing staff about his hobby. 'I was thinking about how cool it would be to bring bees to the White House,' Brandts said. Word made it to chef Sam Kass, who asked Brandts if he could make White House honey to use in Obama family recipes. On the first day of spring, the first beehive was placed in the garden.

✸ Michelle helped plant an organic vegetable garden on the South Lawn of the White House – to educate children about locally grown food, inspiring them to eat healthier and encouraging their families to do the same.

✸ Michelle is the first African–American First Lady

of the United States. 'I'm not supposed to be here, standing here. I'm a statistical oddity. Black girl, brought up on the South Side of Chicago. Was I supposed to go to Princeton? No ... They said maybe Harvard Law was too much for me to reach for. But I went, I did fine. And I'm certainly not supposed to be standing here.'

BARACK AND MICHELLE

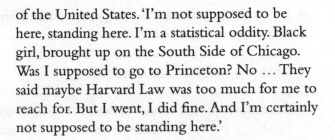

✹ On the night Barack was elected President of the United States of America he had this to say about his wife: 'I would not be standing here tonight without the unyielding support of my best friend for the last 16 years ... the rock of our family, the love of my life, the nation's next First Lady ... Michelle Obama.'

✹ Michelle was expecting Barack to be 'nerdy, strange, off-putting'. But, she says, she was 'pleasantly surprised by who he turned out to be'.

✹ 'I remember that she was tall – almost my height in heels – and lovely, with a friendly, professional manner that matched her tailored suit and blouse,' Obama has said of his first meeting with his wife.

✹ At first, Michelle tried to fix Obama up with her friends, as she wanted their relationship to remain professional. 'They were being careful – or she was,' says John Levi, the partner at Sidley & Austin

who hired them both. 'I gather she was reluctant' to jump into an office romance.

✸ Barack walked up to Michelle one day and said, 'I think we should go out on a date,' but it took another month to convince her.

✸ 'I must say that Barack, about a month in, asked me out. And I thought, No way. This is completely tacky. I've got an advisee and I'm going to date him? So, it took about a month or so for him to talk me into going out on our first date,' she recalled.

✸ This is what Michelle's brother had to say on the subject: 'The first thing I was worried about was, is this poor guy going to make the cut? How long is it going to be until he gets fired? My father was a hard-working man who raised two kids when he had MS, so the example we had was a father full of integrity, and that was the kind of guy my sister was looking for. We used to joke as a family, "She'll never find a guy like that, because they don't exist any more."'

✸ 'I was, like, this guy is different,' Michelle said later. 'He is really different. In addition to being nice and funny and cute and all that, he's got a seriousness and a commitment that you don't see every day.'

✹ Barack 'didn't talk about himself', Michelle's
   mother said. 'He didn't tell us that he was running
   for president of the *Harvard Law Review*. We never
   realised that he was as bright as he is.'

✹ Michelle fell in love with Barack for the same
   reason many other people respect him: his
   connection with people.

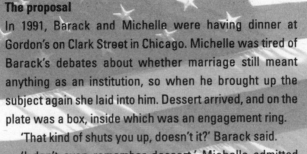

The proposal

In 1991, Barack and Michelle were having dinner at
Gordon's on Clark Street in Chicago. Michelle was tired of
Barack's debates about whether marriage still meant
anything as an institution, so when he brought up the
subject again she laid into him. Dessert arrived, and on the
plate was a box, inside which was an engagement ring.

'That kind of shuts you up, doesn't it?' Barack said.

'I don't even remember dessert,' Michelle admitted
later. 'I don't think I even ate it. I was so shocked and sort
of a little embarrassed because he did sort of shut me up.'

✹ Michelle took her fiancé along to meet a
   potential employer, Valerie Jarrett (now a close
   adviser of Barack's) – not for support, but to see if
   the interviewer met with Barack's approval before
   she accepted the job.

The Wedding

They were married on 10 October 1992 by Reverend Jeremiah A. Wright at Trinity United Church of Christ in Chicago, Illinois. The reception was held at the South Shore Cultural Center.

It was, according to a close friend, 'one of the happier weddings that I had been to, because people understood that putting the two of them together was like putting hydrogen and oxygen together to create this unbelievable life force. Everybody knew it. We understood that together they were going to be so much more than they would have been individually.'

Barack's sister Maya remembers, 'There were everything from the very fair Kansas complexion, you know, the Scots-Irish thing, to the blue-black Kenyan. And we looked like the rainbow tribe – and me in between. I'm Indonesian. The united colours. Never a dull moment, right?'

❋ Barack and Michelle returned to Hawaii almost every Christmas, where his grandmother and sister still lived.

❋ The Obamas had trouble conceiving a child initially, according to Yvonne Davila, Michelle's close friend of 20 years: 'It was hard for her to get pregnant. In fact, I got pregnant first and didn't want to tell her. When she knocked on my door and said, "I'm pregnant!" I cried.'

❋ The couple went through tough times. Barack had to live away from home – in Illinois – during the week while in the State Senate.

❋ After their first daughter, Malia, was born on 4 July 1998, Barack was so busy working that his relationship with Michelle suffered. According to Barack, she was 'pretty fed up with raising our children alone and beginning to question my priorities'. Barack tried to make it a priority to come home from Washington every weekend, from Thursday to Sunday.

❋ Chicago radio host Santita Jackson, daughter of the Reverend Jesse Jackson, is Malia Obama's godmother.

❋ Michelle has said that it's hard being married to a politician, and 'that's why Barack is such a grateful man'.

❋ While on maternity leave with her youngest daughter Sasha, Michelle went to an interview at the University of Chicago medical centre with the baby in a pushchair. 'She really wanted to make that known to me … that family came first,' medical centre president Michael E. Riordan said.

❋ 'I think she defines herself by what is most important to her and I think, at this point in her life, it's raising the girls so that they are

comfortable, safe and happy,' Michelle's close friend Angela Acree has said.

✹ In 2005, Barack and Michelle bought a historic $1.6 million six-bedroom Georgian revival home just blocks from the University of Chicago on the city's South Side.

✹ The Obamas have a family portrait by celebrated portrait photographer Annie Leibovitz which is displayed in a frame turned on its side, because that's the only way it fits.

★ ★ ★ ★ ★ ★ ★ ★ ★ ★ ★ ★ ★ ★

Before the presidential campaign, Barack did the house and car repairs, the chequebook, the grocery shopping and 'I would sometimes do the laundry, although not fold.'

★ ★ ★ ★ ★ ★ ★ ★ ★ ★ ★ ★ ★ ★

✹ Michelle juggled her job as Vice President for Community and External Affairs at the University of Chicago Hospitals with looking after the two girls while Barack was away '98 per cent of the time'.

✹ Michelle would go to the gym before dawn to exercise, so Barack had to dress and feed Malia and Sasha when they woke.

❋ 'Michelle is the one who makes sure all the things that need to get done get done,' said Barack's *Harvard Law* friend Cassandra Butts.

❋ 'My sister is really good at most things,' said Michelle's brother Craig.

❋ Before Barack took to the stage at the 2004 Democratic National Convention, Michelle whispered, 'Don't screw it up, buddy.'

❋ In May 2007, Michelle announced she would quit her job to support her husband's candidacy: 'It's a bit disconcerting,' she said. 'But it's not like I'll be bored.' Michelle campaigned two or three days a week throughout the presidential campaign.

★ ★ ★ ★ ★ ★ ★ ★ ★ ★ ★ ★ ★ ★

During the presidential campaign Michelle complained that Barack didn't put his worn socks in with the dirty clothes, was worse than a five-year-old at making the bed, and left the butter out after breakfast. And that he was 'snore-y and stinky' when he woke up in the morning.

★ ★ ★ ★ ★ ★ ★ ★ ★ ★ ★ ★ ★ ★

❋ 'We have a rule in our house that I can tease and he can't,' Michelle has said.

★ ★ ★ ★ ★ ★ ★ ★ ★ ★ ★ ★ ★ ★

Obama on his wife: 'It is true my wife is smarter, better looking. She's a little meaner than I am.'

★ ★ ★ ★ ★ ★ ★ ★ ★ ★ ★ ★ ★ ★

✹ A *New York Times* columnist wrote that some supporters 'worried that her chiding was emasculating, casting her husband – under fire for lacking experience – as an undisciplined child'.

✹ Michelle does a 90-minute workout three times a week.

✹ She shops at Target, loves *Sex and the City* and never misses the girls' recitals.

✹ 'Sometimes, when we're lying together, I look at her and I feel dizzy with the realisation that here is another distinct person from me, who has memories, origins, thoughts, feelings that are different from my own. That tension between familiarity and mystery meshes something strong between us. Even if one builds a life together based on trust, attentiveness and mutual support, I think that it's important that a partner continues to surprise,' says Obama.

✹ 'Time and love and sacrifice and struggles make you stronger,' says Michelle.

❋ Michelle wants to keep her marriage 'sort of stress-free, free of the discussion, free of the analysis, free of the assessment'.

❋ A senior adviser to the Obamas said the campaign had taken a toll on their love life. 'A quiet dinner date is really special to them,' she said. 'They used to do dinner and a movie but, like every working parent, they're so tired they have to pick either dinner or a movie. If they do both, somebody falls asleep!'

6

Friends of Obama

✷ Obama is the first presidential candidate Oprah Winfrey has endorsed in her whole career. Oprah said she felt compelled to support 'the man I believe has a new vision for America'. She hosted a celebrity-packed fundraiser at her California home that amassed an estimated $3 million.

✷ 'My money isn't going to make any difference,' said Oprah. 'My value to him, my support of him is probably worth more than any other cheque that I could write.'

★ ★ ★ ★ ★ ★ ★ ★ ★ ★ ★ ★ ★ ★

Obama has been known to refer to Oprah as 'my girl'. And she likes to refer to him as 'my favourite guy' and 'my choice'.

★ ★ ★ ★ ★ ★ ★ ★ ★ ★ ★ ★ ★ ★

✷ *Friends* icon Jennifer Aniston donated $2,300 to Obama's campaign.

✷ Robert De Niro endorsed Barack at a New Jersey fundraiser and has defended him against allegations of inexperience, saying that a candidate who hadn't taken his country into war had 'the kind of inexperience I can get used to'.

✷ Tom Hanks endorsed Barack on YouTube, and Neil Young mentioned Barack Obama in the lyric to his 2006 song 'Lookin' for a Leader'.

★ ★ ★ ★ ★ ★ ★ ★ ★ ★ ★ ★ ★ ★ ★

A 34-year-old named Dale Lee Bishop, who was a participant in the 1998 claw-hammer homicide of an acquaintance, endorsed Obama just before he was executed.

★ ★ ★ ★ ★ ★ ★ ★ ★ ★ ★ ★ ★ ★ ★

❋ During a concert held by Billy Joel and Bruce Springsteen, Bruce turned from the crowd and returned on stage with none other than presidential candidate Barack Obama, introduced as 'the next President of the United States'.

❋ Will Smith said, 'I just gave him a call and asked him to tell me to go where he thought he needed me. I think he's what the future of America is going to be. Barack represents what I feel is the future of the optimum survival of America.'

❋ Stevie Wonder said of Barack: 'He's a combination of JFK and Martin Luther King. With that he can't lose.'

❋ Caroline Kennedy Schlossberg – the only surviving child of John F Kennedy – caused a frenzy by writing 'A President Like My Father' for the *New York Times*, comparing her dad's inspirational qualities with Obama's.

✸ Maria Shriver, a member of the Kennedy clan and wife of the Republican California Governor Arnold Schwarzenegger, plumped for Obama despite her McCain-endorsing husband.

★ ★ ★ ★ ★ ★ ★ ★ ★ ★ ★ ★ ★ ★

Scarlett Johansson sang in the 'Yes We Can' video, recorded phone messages and campaigned in Iowa. She joked she was 'engaged to Barack Obama'.

★ ★ ★ ★ ★ ★ ★ ★ ★ ★ ★ ★ ★ ★

✸ *The Other Boleyn Girl* Natalie Portman endorsed Hillary Clinton.

✸ George Clooney is a self-proclaimed 'Obama guy'. He says Obama has the 'aura of a rock star'. He appeared with Obama on a panel on Darfur in 2006 and has often voiced support, although he says celebrity endorsements can do more harm than good.

✸ Ben Affleck and his wife Jennifer Garner threw a glitzy fundraiser for Obama. 'Hollywood loves Obama,' said Ben.

✸ Veteran folk singer Joan Baez, whose protest songs became famous alongside the likes of Bob Dylan in the Greenwich Village folk scene of the early 1960s, threw her support behind Obama.

✸ *Bourne Identity* star Matt Damon said, 'It is very important for me to do what I can to help the Obama campaign so people will go out and vote. We need change in this country and now is the time to be sure that happens.'

✸ Halle Berry was seen out and about sporting a 'Barack The Vote!' T-shirt.

✸ Samuel L. Jackson skipped the Academy Awards to campaign for Obama in Texas. 'We need somebody the world relates to in a very real kind of way.' He donated $4,300 to Barack's election campaign.

✸ Other fans include: Jamie Foxx, Beyoncé Knowles, Jay-Z, Ben Stiller, Bono, Ed Norton, Tobey Maguire and Eddie Murphy.

Obama ~ Round the World

BARACK IN THE UK

✵ Barack is the 13th-generation descendant of Deacon Thomas Blossom, a 17th-century Pilgrim settler who emigrated from England to America as one of the founding fathers of the colony of Plymouth, Massachusetts.

His distant cousin, Charles Blossom, is a former lecturer in automotive engineering at Loughborough University.

✵ Kezia Obama, Obama Sr's first wife, lives in Bracknell in England, where Kezia moved to be near her daughter Auma – Barack's half-sister. Barack and Kezia have met in both America and Bracknell.

✵ The President's half-sister Auma lives in London. Obama was at Auma's fiancé's stag do ten years ago, which involved a stripping policewoman and a tour of Wokingham's pubs and working men's clubs.

★ ★ ★ ★ ★ ★ ★ ★ ★ ★ ★ ★ ★ ★

Barack removed a bust of Sir Winston Churchill from the Oval Office. The bust was loaned to George W. Bush from the Government's art collection after the September 11th attacks, but was formally handed back once Obama took over. A bust of Abraham Lincoln now sits in the Oval Office.

★ ★ ★ ★ ★ ★ ★ ★ ★ ★ ★ ★ ★ ★

✤ Gordon Brown was the first European leader to meet President Obama after his inauguration. 'I've come here to renew our special relationship for new times. It's a partnership of purpose. It's a partnership of purpose that is born out of shared values. It's a partnership of purpose that is founded on a determination to rise to every challenge. And it's a partnership of purpose that is driven forward now by the need for us all to work together in unity to deal with the world economic problems,' said Mr Brown.

★ ★ ★ ★ ★ ★ ★ ★ ★ ★ ★ ★ ★ ★

British PM Gordon Brown gave Obama an ornamental pen holder made from the timbers of the Victorian ship HMS Gannet, which was used in anti-slavery patrols alongside its sister ship the HMS Resolute. The desk in the White House Oval office is built from the timbers of the HMS Resolute and is called the 'Resolute desk'.

★ ★ ★ ★ ★ ★ ★ ★ ★ ★ ★ ★ ★ ★

✤ Barack gave Gordon a box of DVDs, including *ET*, *The Wizard of Oz* and *Star Wars*. The only problem was that the Prime Minister was unable to watch them – the discs were made in North America and wouldn't work on Brown's European DVD player.

✤ The Queen invited the President to tea while attending the G20 summit in the UK. During the G20 reception, the Queen broke Royal protocol by putting a friendly arm around Michelle Obama's waist when she found herself next to the first lady and remarked on their height difference. Michelle returned the gesture. It was the first time in Her Majesty's long public life that she has put her arm around another woman. A Buckingham Palace spokesperson described the moment as 'a mutual and spontaneous display of affection'.

British bookmaker William Hill is offering odds on Michelle having a baby in her husband's first term in office. They also have odds on Obama winning a second term of office, capturing Bin Laden, winning a Nobel Prize, buying a White House cat, changing the constitution to allow three presidential terms, and attending a Premier League game.

OBAMA AND KENYA

* Mama Sarah, Obama's step-grandmother, lives in Kogelo without electricity or running water. Sarah is illiterate and doesn't know when she was born. She and Obama communicate using an interpreter.

* During his campaign Obama drew support from the Luo ethnic group of his ancestors in Kenya, while many members of the rival Kikuyu group supported Hillary Clinton.

* Obama's grandfather was the first black person in

his Kenyan clan to wear Western clothes rather than just a loincloth, and among the first who learned to speak, read and write English.

★ ★ ★ ★ ★ ★ ★ ★ ★ ★ ★ ★ ★ ★

Kenyan relatives celebrated Obama's election by slaughtering a bull named Barack Hussein Obama in his honour. Mama Sarah chanted, 'We're going to the White House! We're going to the White House!'

★ ★ ★ ★ ★ ★ ★ ★ ★ ★ ★ ★ ★ ★

✳ Some of Obama's relatives arranged bus tours to bring visitors to have tea with Obama's step-grandmother Sarah.

✳ The government in Nairobi declared the day Obama was elected a public holiday.

OBAMA AND IRELAND

✳ Obama is 3.1 per cent Irish. His great-great-grandfather lived in Moneygall in Co. Offaly, an hour west of Dublin, until he emigrated to America in 1850.

✳ 'It turns out I have Irish heritage, and I'm not talking about my cousin Dick Cheney,' Obama told a crowd at a St Patrick's Day dinner in Scranton, Pennsylvania last year. 'It never hurts to be a little Irish when running for President of the United States.'

✹ An estimated 30 million Americans claim Irish ancestry.

✹ He has an Irish eighth cousin called Henry Healy.

✹ During the election campaign, Irish band the Corrigan Brothers had a hit with humorous folk song 'There's No One as Irish as Barack O'Bama'.

✹ Barack is committed to peace in Northern Ireland: 'The determined optimism of the Irish people has enabled them to grab hold of hope in the United States, from South Boston to the south side of Chicago. It's an optimism expressed in three issues so important to Irish-Americans today: a lasting peace in Northern Ireland, an American immigration policy that keeps faith with our tradition of offering opportunity to those who seek it, and strong economic and cultural ties between our two nations. Not all Americans are Irish but all Americans support those who stand on the side of peace and peace will prevail.'

✹ Irish rock group U2 performed at Obama's inauguration. 'This is not just an American dream, but also an Irish dream, a European dream, an African dream, an Israeli dream and a Palestinian

dream,' Bono said in the middle of their 1984 hit 'Pride (In the Name of Love)'.

❀ Barack continues the tradition of welcoming the Irish Prime Minister to the White House on St Patrick's Day.

❀ Obama hosted a lavish dinner party for 400 guests in the Irish Prime Minister's honour to mark St Patrick's Day.

❀ Obama joked to the Irish Premier Brian Cowen, 'We may be cousins. We haven't sorted that through yet.'

❀ Guests at the St Patrick's Day cocktail reception drank green sparkling wine.

❀ The Irish Prime Minister's after-dinner speech began 'by welcoming a strong friend of the United States' before he quickly realised he was reading Obama's speech.

❀ The water in the fountains on the north and south lawns of the White House was dyed green to mark the national holiday of Ireland. It was Michelle Obama's idea – she was inspired by the St Patrick's Day celebrations in her hometown of Chicago, where the city marks the holiday by dyeing the river green.

OBAMA AND IRAN

✹ According to Barack, Iran is a threat to all of us. 'There's no greater threat to Israel or to the peace and stability of the region than Iran,' he said on 4 June 2008.

✹ Obama believes global leaders must do whatever it takes to stop Iran from enriching uranium and acquiring nuclear weapons.

✹ Barack has said that Iranian President Mahmoud Ahmadinejad is 'reckless, irresponsible and inattentive' to the needs of the Iranian people, but in 2009 added, 'If countries like Iran are willing to unclench their fists, they will find an extended hand from us.'

✹ He believes the United States should engage in 'aggressive diplomacy combined with tough sanctions' to stop Iran becoming a nuclear threat.

✹ 'Tough but engaged diplomacy' is what's needed, according to the President.

✹ President Obama issued a video appeal to Iran in 2009, to mark the start of Nowruz, the Iranian New Year, offering a 'new beginning' of diplomatic engagement. He wanted to 'speak directly to the people and leaders of the Islamic

Republic of Iran' to tell them that he was committed to establishing 'constructive ties'.

❋ 'My administration is now committed to diplomacy that addresses the full range of issues before us, and to pursuing constructive ties among the United States, Iran and the international community ... This process will not be advanced by threats. We seek instead engagement that is honest and grounded in mutual respect.'

❋ Iran should use its 'true greatness' to create rather than destroy, he warned. 'You have that right [to take a place in the world] – but it comes with real responsibilities, and that place cannot be reached through terror or arms, but rather through peaceful actions that demonstrate the true greatness of the Iranian people and civilisation.'

OBAMA AND IRAQ

❋ The Iraq war has strengthened Iran's influence in the region, said Obama, producing 'anti-US and further anti-Israel propaganda'.

❋ President Obama plans to withdraw most troops from Iraq by 2010. Up to 50,000 of 142,000 troops will stay on in Iraq until the end of 2011, to advise Iraqi forces and protect US interests.

✺ 'The drawdown of our military should send a clear signal that Iraq's future is now its own responsibility,' Obama said.

✺ In a speech to Marines, Barack said, 'Iraq is not yet secure, and there will be difficult days ahead. Violence will continue to be a part of life in Iraq. Too many fundamental political questions about Iraq's future remain unresolved. Too many Iraqis are still displaced or destitute.'

✺ 'I support President Obama for taking a step in the right direction in Iraq, but I do not think that his plan goes far enough,' said Democratic Representative Dennis Kucinich. 'You cannot leave combat troops in a foreign country to conduct combat operations and call it the end of the war. You can't be in and out at the same time.'

OBAMA AND AFGHANISTAN

✺ Obama ordered a further 17,000 US troops into Afghanistan, to bring the American presence there up to 50,000. 'This increase is necessary to stabilise a deteriorating situation in Afghanistan, which has not received the strategic attention, direction and resources it urgently requires,' he said.

✸ 'Afghanistan is still winnable,' claims Obama, 'in the sense of our ability to ensure that it is not a launching pad for attacks against North America.'

✸ His objective: 'to stamp out al-Qaeda to make sure that extremism is not expanding but rather is contracting'.

✸ 'We don't have a choice; we've got to finish the job,' said the President.

OBAMA AND ISRAEL AND PALESTINE

✸ 'I think that the idea of a secure Jewish state is a fundamentally just idea, and a necessary idea, given not only world history but the active existence of anti-Semitism, the potential vulnerability that the Jewish people could still experience.'

✸ Obama promised to work towards ending the Israeli–Palestinian conflict 'from the minute I'm sworn into office'.

✸ When asked to comment on Israel's attack on Gaza, Obama said, 'If missiles were falling where my two daughters sleep, I would do everything in order to stop that.'

❋ The Hamas leader Ahmed Yousef said, 'We like Mr Obama and we hope that he will win the election.'

❋ Obama on Hamas: 'They are a terrorist organisation and I've repeatedly condemned them. I've repeatedly said, and I mean what I say: Since they are a terrorist organisation, we should not be dealing with them until they recognise Israel, renounce terrorism, and abide by previous agreements.'

Obama's Family

⁕ Malia was born in 1998, and Sasha was born in 2001.

⁕ The Obamas are strict parents. They insist that, at least for breakfast, Malia and Sasha eat only organic produce.

⁕ The couple have received advice from past First Ladies Laura Bush, Rosalyn Carter and Hillary Rodham Clinton about raising children in the White House.

⁕ 'Michelle is an extraordinary mother to our two girls. She works every day to instil in our girls the same values we were raised with,' Obama says.

Obama's daughters are given an allowance of $1 a week for household chores. Chores include: making their own bed ('Doesn't have to look good – just throw the sheet over it,' Michelle says), getting themselves up in the morning, keeping the playroom toy closet clean, setting and clearing the dinner table, lights out by 8.30pm, and 'No whining, arguing or annoying teasing.'

⁕ Sasha and Malia are only allowed to watch one hour of television a day.

⁕ They are still expected to do chores now they are

in the White House. 'That was the first thing I said to the staff,' says Michelle, '"You know, we're going to have to set up some boundaries," because they're going to need to be able to make their beds and clean up.'

❋ The girls don't receive birthday or Christmas gifts from their parents, who spend 'hundreds' on birthday slumber parties instead. As Barack put it, 'We want to teach some limits.'

❋ Malia once said, 'I know there is a Santa because there's no way they'd buy me all that stuff!'

❋ Michelle's 72-year-old mother Marian Robinson cared for Malia and Sasha during the presidential campaign and will live in the White House with the first family. Marian has been dubbed the 'First Granny'.

❋ Their grandmother is a little lax in enforcing their parents' rules. She has said that the girl's 8.30pm bedtime is ridiculous, and called her daughter Michelle's rules 'going overboard'. 'I have candy, they stay up late,' Granny Robinson says. 'They watch television for as long as they want to. We'll play games until the wee hours. I do everything that grandmothers do that they're not supposed to … But don't tell Barack because he cannot stand TV watching.'

✻ Malia plays football, and attends dance and drama lessons, and Sasha does gymnastics and tap dancing. They both practise the piano every day.

✻ Many mornings the girls climb into their parents' bed.

✻ Malia and Sasha are two of the youngest residents in the White House for more than 30 years, since Amy Carter moved in at the age of nine in 1977.

✻ Malia told her father, 'I'm going to sit at that desk [in the Lincoln Room at the White House], because it will inspire big thoughts.'

✻ The girls have the run of 18 acres of grounds and 132 rooms, including a cinema, a swimming pool, a solarium and a tenpin bowling alley.

✻ Malia said before they moved in: 'My most excitement about it is that I get to redecorate my room. I get to get this whole new room and do whatever I want.'

✻ Obama promised the girls a dog if they got into the White House. 'They say if you want a friend in Washington, get a dog,' Obama joked. But Malia is allergic to animal dander, so the choice was narrowed down to either a labradoodle or a Portuguese Water Dog.

Obama's Family

★ ★ ★ ★ ★ ★ ★ ★ ★ ★ ★ ★ ★ ★ ★

In April 2009, a six-month-old Portuguese Water Dog named Bo took up residence as the Obama's dog in the White House. Malia and Sasha chose the name because their cousins have a cat named Bo and because Michelle's father was nicknamed 'Diddley' after Bo Diddley.

★ ★ ★ ★ ★ ★ ★ ★ ★ ★ ★ ★ ★ ★ ★

✺ The dog was a gift from Senator Ted Kennedy, who owns three dogs of the same breed.

✺ Before his inauguration, President Obama published an open letter to his daughters, describing what he wanted for them and every child in America: 'to grow up in a world with no limits on your dreams and no achievements beyond your reach, and to grow into compassionate, committed women who will help build that world'.

✺ The Obama girls began at Sidwell Friends, a private Quaker school in Washington on 5 January 2009. It's where Chelsea Clinton was educated. Before moving to Washington they attended a private school called the University of Chicago Lab School.

✺ Barack says of his job, 'If I ever thought this was ruining my family, I wouldn't do it.'

Sporty Obama

✹ Obama is 'a big sports nut', according to a campaign source.

✹ 'We go play hoop,' was Obama's message in his final high-school yearbook.

✹ Barack has plans to rip out the indoor bowling alley at the White House and install a basketball court.

✹ 'I dream of playing basketball,' said Obama when asked, hours before his presidential victory, what had occupied his mind as he slept on the eve of the election.

✹ The President was nicknamed Barry O'Bomber at high school in Hawaii because of his devastating 'jump shot' and would dribble and bounce a ball as he walked between classes.

✹ He struggled to make the starting line-up of his champion school team.

★ ★ ★ ★ ★ ★ ★ ★ ★ ★ ★ ★ ★ ★
**During the 21-month election campaign, Obama made
a point of playing a game of basketball every election day.**
★ ★ ★ ★ ★ ★ ★ ★ ★ ★ ★ ★ ★ ★

✹ Arne Duncan, Obama's Education Secretary, is a 6ft 5in-tall former co-captain of Harvard's basketball team. He also played professionally in Australia. 'I just want to dispel one rumour before I take questions. I did not select Arne because he's one of the best basketball players I know,' Barack has said. 'Although I will say that I think we are putting together the best basketball-playing cabinet in American history. And I think that is worth noting.'

✸ The United Nations Ambassador, Susan Rice, is just 5ft 3in tall but was a star basketball player at National Cathedral School in Washington, where she was nicknamed Spo – short for Sporting.

✸ General James Jones, 64, the National Security Adviser, stands at 6ft 4in and was a forward for the Georgetown University Basketball team, the Hoyas.

✸ Eric Holder, 57, the Attorney General, was co-captain of the Peglegs, his high-school basketball team in New York and also played at Columbia University.

✸ Mr Volcker, chairman of the President's Economic Recovery Advisory Board, is 6ft 7in, and played basketball for Princeton.

✸ Obama played basketball with US troops in Afghanistan in 2008.

✹ Barack works out in the gym nearly every day.

✹ His adopted home city of Chicago is one of the contenders for the 2016 Olympic Games.

✹ Obama is a fan of the White Sox baseball team.

✹ 'Obama's interest in sports and specifically in baseball, combined with the efforts of other world leaders, is the kind of thing we need to return baseball to the Olympic programme,' the International Baseball Federation President Harvey Schiller said.

✹ Barack grew up playing football in Indonesia. When he returned to America, he was dismayed to discover that kids his age didn't play football: 'Nobody played soccer or badminton or chess, and I had no idea how to throw a football in a spiral or balance on a skateboard.'

✹ Obama's daughter plays football every weekend, and Barack goes along to support her when he can.

✹ Obama is a West Ham United fan. He watches Premier League games whenever his schedule allows.

✹ 'I think it is about time we had playoffs in college football,' Obama says. 'I'm fed up with these

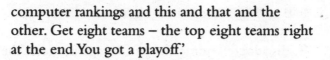

computer rankings and this and that and the other. Get eight teams – the top eight teams right at the end. You got a playoff.'

❋ Obama is a left-handed golfer.

❋ Tiger Woods wants to play golf with Barack Obama, according to a newsletter posted on the golfer's website.

❋ When asked by Jay Leno about his bowling at the Whitehouse Alley, Obama said, 'I have been practising … I bowled a 129.'
   'That's very good, Mr President,' said Leno, to which Obama replied, 'It's like – it was like the Special Olympics, or something.'
   Although neither Leno nor Obama seemed bothered by the comment during the show, the White House issued a statement apologising for it before the show aired.

❋ Barack dabbles in a bit of bodysurfing while on holidays in Hawaii.

❋ Poker is one of Obama's hidden talents. He says himself he's a 'pretty good' player. He was one of the founders of a senators' poker night at Capitol Hill: 'It's a fun way for people to relax and share stories and give each other a hard time over friendly competition. In Springfield, it was a way

to get to know other senators including Republicans.'

✸ Obama was known as a cautious poker player with a good poker face. 'When Barack stayed in, you pretty much figured he'd got a good hand,' noted a former senator.

10

Obama and the Big Issues

THE ECONOMY

❋ Obama believes that if the government doesn't act quickly the recession will last for years.

The White House stated it would team with investors to initially buy as much as $1 trillion in bad assets from banks reluctant to make loans.

❋ Barack put forth a £75 billion American Recovery and Reinvestment Plan:

- To double the production of alternative energy over three years.
- To modernise some 75 per cent of federal buildings and improve the energy efficiency of two million American homes.
- To ensure that all of America's medical records are computerised within five years.
- To update classrooms, labs and libraries in tens of thousands of schools, community colleges and public universities.
- To expand broadband across America, so that small rural businesses can compete with the rest of the world.
- To invest in science, research and technology that will lead to new medical breakthroughs and new industries.

❋ Seeking to boost the US clean-energy industry, President Obama announced $1.2 billion for science research at national labs and a proposal to extend a business tax credit for investments in research and development.

FOREIGN POLICY

❋ The greatest threat to national security, according to Obama, is the resurgence of al Qaeda and the Taliban in Afghanistan and Pakistan.

❋ Barack plans to increase troops in Afghanistan, encouraging the members of NATO to do the same.

❋ The President has demanded the Afghan government crack down on corruption and the illicit opium trade.

❋ Obama intends to increase non-military aid to Pakistan and hold them accountable for security in the border region with Afghanistan.

❋ Obama wants to see the world rid of nuclear weapons, and plans to negotiate a global ban on the production of new nuclear weapons material.

❋ Barack wants to strengthen the Nuclear Non-Proliferation Treaty so that countries that break the rules, like North Korea and Iran, will face strong international sanctions.

❋ He supports tough and direct diplomacy with

Iran. If it abandons its nuclear programme and support for terrorism, the US will offer incentives like membership of the World Trade Organisation and economic investments; if not, the US will step up its economic pressure and political isolation.

❋ During the July 2006 Lebanon war, Obama supported Israel's right to defend itself from Hezbollah, insisting that Israel should not be pressured into a ceasefire that did not deal with the threat of Hezbollah missiles.

❋ He has called for continuing US cooperation with Israel in the development of missile defence systems.

❋ Obama intends to work with Israelis and Palestinians to achieve a Jewish state in Israel and a Palestinian state, living side by side in peace and security.

❋ Barack plans to end the US's combat mission in Iraq by 31 August 2010.

❋ The forces that remain will be there to train, equip and advise the Iraqi Security Forces, conduct targeted counterterrorism operations and provide protection for military and civilian personnel. All troops are planned to be removed by the end of 2011.

❋ The United States will try to renew diplomatic relations with all nations in the Middle East, including Iran and Syria. Obama sent a video greeting to the people of Iran for Persian New Year, making it clear that he was seeking a change in Iranian behaviour rather than a change in the regime. 'On the occasion of your new year, I want you, the people and leaders of Iran, to understand the future that we seek. It's a future with renewed exchanges among our people, and greater opportunities for partnership and commerce,' said the President. 'It's a future where the old divisions are overcome, where you and all of your neighbours and the wider world can live in greater security and greater peace.'

❋ President Obama has been a leading voice in Washington urging the end of genocide in Sudan. He travelled to the United Nations to meet with Sudanese officials and visited refugee camps on the Chad–Sudan border to raise international awareness of the ongoing humanitarian disaster there. He also worked to secure $20 million for the African Union peacekeeping mission to Darfur.

SEX & GENDER

❋ 'It's the right thing to do ... to provide age-appropriate sex education, science-based education in schools.'

✳ 'The fact is, my nine-year-old and my six-year-old I think are already aware that there are same-sex couples. One of the things I want to communicate to my children is not to be afraid of people who are different.'

✳ A fake Obama sex video spam was released in 2008 containing spy software.

✳ Barack Obama supported gay rights during his Illinois Senate tenure. He sponsored legislation that would ban discrimination on the basis of sexual orientation.

★ ★ ★ ★ ★ ★ ★ ★ ★ ★ ★ ★ ★ ★

In 2006, the Human Rights Campaign, the largest national gay and lesbian organisation in the US, issued Obama with a scorecard of 89 out of 100 on his sponsorship and voting on key issues of importance to gay and lesbian citizens.

★ ★ ★ ★ ★ ★ ★ ★ ★ ★ ★ ★ ★ ★

✳ President Obama believes that the US anti-discrimination employment laws should be expanded to include sexual orientation and gender identity.

✳ Obama thinks that the government needs to repeal the 'don't ask, don't tell' policy towards sexual orientation in the military.

★ ★ ★ ★ ★ ★ ★ ★ ★ ★ ★ ★ ★ ★ ★

The President believes that adoption should be an option for all couples and individuals, regardless of their sexual orientation. He thinks that a child will benefit from a healthy and loving home, whether the parents are gay or not.

★ ★ ★ ★ ★ ★ ★ ★ ★ ★ ★ ★ ★ ★ ★

✸ Barack supports civil unions that give same-sex couples legal rights and privileges equal to those of married couples, but is against gay marriage. 'I'm a Christian. And so, although I try not to have my religious beliefs dominate or determine my political views on this issue, I do believe that tradition and my religious beliefs say that marriage is something sanctified between a man and a woman.'

✸ Obama is pro-abortion. One of the first things he did as President was overturn a ban on federal funding for foreign family planning agencies that promote or give information about abortion.

✸ Barack is a co-sponsor of the Stem Cell Research Enhancement Act of 2007, which will allow research of human embryonic stem cells derived from embryos donated from in vitro fertilisation clinics.

✸ Obama co-sponsored legislation to expand access to contraception, health information, and preventative services to help reduce unintended pregnancies.

RACE

❋ Obama is the son of a black man from Kenya and a white woman from Kansas.

❋ He is married to a black American who is descended from slaves and slave owners.

❋ Barack has been criticised by some for being 'too black' and by others for not being 'black enough'. Responding to the question of whether he is 'black enough', Obama said, 'We're still locked in this notion that if you appeal to white folks then there must be something wrong.'

❋ Barack wants to increase the number of legal immigrants to keep families together and meet the demand for jobs that employers cannot fill.

❋ He also wants to support a system that allows illegal immigrants who are in good standing to pay a fine, learn English and join the queue for the opportunity to become citizens.

❋ He encourages the promotion of economic development in Mexico to decrease illegal immigration.

RELIGION

❋ Obama's mother was Christian-turned-agnostic and his father Muslim-turned-atheist.

✸ Barack's father considered religion 'mumbo jumbo'.

✸ His mother occasionally took him to Catholic mass while in Indonesia. She also took him to Borobudur, one of the largest Buddhist temples in the world.

✸ While working in India, his mother lived for a time in a Buddhist monastery.

✸ His stepfather 'followed a brand of Islam that could make room for the remnants of more ancient animist and Hindu faiths'. He explained to Obama 'that a man took on the powers of whatever he ate'.

★ ★ ★ ★ ★ ★ ★ ★ ★ ★ ★ ★ ★ ★
In Indonesia, Obama saw Muslims living comfortably next to Christians, showing him that 'Islam can be compatible with the modern world'.
★ ★ ★ ★ ★ ★ ★ ★ ★ ★ ★ ★ ★ ★

✸ Back in Hawaii his family celebrated Easter and Christmas.

✸ Barack lived 'an ascetic existence' while at Columbia University: 'I did a lot of spiritual exploration.'

the Barack Obama Miscellany

★ ★ ★ ★ ★ ★ ★ ★ ★ ★ ★ ★ ★ ★ ★

Barack used to fast, and would often go for days without speaking to another person.

★ ★ ★ ★ ★ ★ ★ ★ ★ ★ ★ ★ ★ ★ ★

✴ He read Saint Augustine, Friedrich Nietzsche and Graham Greene.

✴ Some Sunday mornings he would wander into an African-American congregation such as the Abyssinian Baptist Church in Harlem.

✴ Barack was baptised in the early 1990s at Trinity United Church of Christ in Chicago.

✴ As newly weds, Barack and Michelle went to church two or three times a month, but that became less frequent after their first child was born.

✴ His daughters, Malia and Sasha, have not attended Sunday school.

✴ The family says grace at mealtime, and he talks to the children about God whenever they have questions.

✴ Barack prays every day, for 'forgiveness for my sins and flaws, which are many, the protection of my family, and that I'm carrying out God's will, not in a grandiose way, but simply that there is an alignment between my actions and what he would want'.

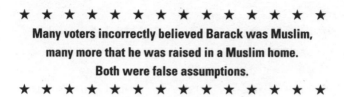

★ ★ ★ ★ ★ ★ ★ ★ ★ ★ ★ ★ ★ ★ ★

Many voters incorrectly believed Barack was Muslim, many more that he was raised in a Muslim home. Both were false assumptions.

★ ★ ★ ★ ★ ★ ★ ★ ★ ★ ★ ★ ★ ★ ★

DRUGS

✹ Obama is steering drug policy towards prevention and 'harm reduction' rather than 'war on drugs'.

✹ The Obama administration will support federally funded needle exchanges. 'With escalating violence along our Southwest border and far too many suffering from addiction here at home, never has it been more important to have a national drug-control strategy guided by sound principles of public safety and public health,' says the President.

★ ★ ★ ★ ★ ★ ★ ★ ★ ★ ★ ★ ★ ★ ★

Barack has admitted to dabbling in marijuana and alcohol, and sometimes cocaine at high school. His high-school yearbook picture inscription thanks 'Tut', 'Gramps' and the 'Choom Gang'. Choom is Hawaiian slang for 'pot smoking'.

★ ★ ★ ★ ★ ★ ★ ★ ★ ★ ★ ★ ★ ★ ★

✻ Barack's half-brother, George Obama, was arrested for possession of marijuana after being caught with a single joint near his home in a Nairobi slum in 2009. The charge was dropped.

✻ Barack promised his wife he'd kick his smoking habit if he stood for the White House, but he fell off the wagon on the campaign trail.

Obama Humour

Q Why won't Obama laugh at himself?
A Because it would be racist.

✹ Bill Maher recently joked, 'Barack Obama has to give comedians something to work with. Seriously, here's a guy who's not fat, not cheating on his wife, not stupid, not angry and not a phony. Who needs an a★★hole like that around for the next four years?!'

   He went on to joke that he doesn't want to have to shy away from jokes at Obama's expense for the next four years for fear of being dubbed a racist: 'If you can't laugh at a guy who went to Columbia, Harvard, the Senate and the White House, and who happens to be black, the racist is you.'

✹ Harry Truman said, 'The buck stops here!'
Barack Obama says, 'Leave the bucks here!'

Q Why is Barack Obama so thin and scrawny?
A If he were any heavier he wouldn't be able to walk on water.

Q How many Obamas does it take to change a light bulb?
A Only one, but it has to be a change the light bulb can believe in.

✹ Anagrams
President Barack Hussein Obama =
A Democrat speaks inane rubbish

Q Why did Jay Leno vote for Barack Obama?
A Because he was running out of George Bush jokes.

Q Why did David Letterman vote for Barack Obama?
A Because he was running out of Jay Leno's George Bush jokes.

Q What's the problem with Barack Obama jokes?
A His followers don't think they're funny and other people don't think they're jokes.

Q Why did John McCain cross the road?
A There was an Old Town Buffet on the other side.

Q Why did Barack Obama cross the road?
A To help the other side.

✹ 'Shocking news out of Illinois today. Governor Rod Blagojevich was arrested on corruption charges, including the allegation that he was selling Barack Obama's vacant Senate seat. Now, I personally am surprised Obama even needed a seat. I thought he just levitated.' – *Stephen Colbert*

✹ 'This is a true story. Some people alongside Barack Obama's inaugural parade route got bored

waiting for it to start. So, did you see this? They started doing the electric slide. Yeah, apparently, the best way to celebrate our first black President is to do the whitest dance imaginable.'
– *Conan O'Brien*

✳ 'Barack Obama's mother-in-law might be moving into the White House with him. Joe Biden was right. Hostile forces will test him in the first few months.' – *Jay Leno*

✳ 'Oprah Winfrey just announced that she's planning to attend Barack Obama's inauguration. Oprah says she's very excited to see Obama become the second-most powerful person in the world.' – *Conan O'Brien*

✳ Last night was the final Democratic debate … I guess one of the big stories was that Barack Obama had a little bit of trouble last night. He is so smooth and he's so good, but last night he had a little trouble. Last night, during the debate, Barack Obama mispronounced the word "Massachusetts" twice and then mispronounced the word "filibuster". Which explains why this morning Obama was endorsed by President Bush.' – *Conan O'Brien*

✳ 'You know. People really like Barack Obama because he's an inspirational speaker. But he was not the first one – I was checking my presidential history – he was not the first candidate to use the phrase "Yes we can!" Bill Clinton frequently used that on interns.' – *David Letterman*

'Jesse Jackson also said he thought Barack Obama was talking down to black people by lecturing on things like fatherhood and being a responsible husband. Jesse thought it was insulting, not only to him, but to his former mistress and their lovechild.' – *Jay Leno*

'After a quick meet-and-greet with King Abdullah, Obama was off to Israel, where he made a quick stop at the manger in Bethlehem where he was born.' – *Jon Stewart, on Barack Obama's Middle East trip*

'At a rally in Florida, Barack Obama was interrupted by a protest group calling themselves "Blacks Against Obama". Actually, a pretty small group. It's just Condoleezza Rice and Jesse Jackson.' – *Jay Leno*

'Barack Obama said today the government's $700 billion bailout should not be a blank cheque. Barack Obama says he knows that $700 billion is a lot of money. In fact, it would take him at least ten Hollywood fundraisers to come up with that kind of money.' – *Jay Leno*

✺ 'Senator Barack Obama proposed for the first time setting a deadline for withdrawing troops from Iraq, as part of a broader plan aimed at bolstering his foreign policy credentials. Because if you don't know your foreign policy, you might only get elected President twice.' – *Amy Poehler*

✺ 'Ladies and gentlemen, Barack Obama is our new President. And I think I speak for most Americans when I say, anybody mind if he starts a little early?' – *David Letterman*

✺ 'You notice that people who've been in Washington too long, they don't talk like ordinary folks. We had this debate in Las Vegas, and somebody asked me, "What are your weaknesses?" So I said, "Well, you know, I don't keep track of paper that well, I'm always losing paper, my desk is a mess." And then they asked the next two candidates. And one candidate says, "Well, my biggest weakness is I'm just so passionate about helping poor people." And then the other one says, "I'm just so impatient to help the American people solve their problems." So then I realise, well, I wish I'd gone last and then I would have known. I'm stupid that way, I thought that when they asked what your biggest weakness was, they asked what your biggest weakness was. And now I know that my biggest weakness is I like to help old ladies across the street.' – *Barack Obama*

❋ 'Now that's my phone buzzing there. I don't
want you to think I'm getting fresh or anything.'
– *Barack Obama posing for a picture with supporters
in Indiana, when he apparently felt his phone start
to vibrate in his pocket, against which one woman was
closely pressed*

❋ 'Look, when I was a kid, I inhaled frequently.
That was the point.' – *Barack Obama*

12

Obama Family Ties

✳ Obama's maternal heritage consists mostly of English ancestry, with much smaller amounts of German, Irish, Scottish, Welsh, Swiss and French ancestry.

✳ Obama is descended from the Pilgrim Fathers who left the Dutch town of Leiden in 1620 to found the Plymouth colony in Massachusetts. He is the seventh American President directly descended from the Pilgrim Fathers.

Republican Relatives

George W. Bush and Obama are tenth cousins once removed – linked through a 17th-century Massachusetts couple, Samuel Hinckley and Sarah Soole. In response to the news that Dick Cheney and Barack Obama are 11th cousins, a spokesperson from the Obama camp joked, 'Every family has a black sheep.' Their shared ancestors are Mareen and Susannah Duvall, 17th-century immigrants from France.

✳ Brad Pitt is Obama's ninth cousin.

✳ Barack also has family lines to Presidents James Madison, Harry Truman, Lyndon Johnson, Gerald Ford and Jimmy Carter; and 19th-century cowboy Wild Bill Hickok.

❋ Obama's great-great-great-great-grandfather, George Washington Overall, owned a 15-year-old girl and a 25-year-old man.

❋ One of Obama's great-great-great-great-great-grandmothers, Mary Duvall, also owned two black slaves – a 60-year-old man and a 58-year-old woman.

❋ Obama is also eligible for membership in the Sons of the American Revolution, as his great-great-great-grandfather Robert Wolfey who served in the Ohio Infantry during the Civil War. Family rumours also say he is distantly related to Jefferson Davis, President of the Confederacy.

❋ Obama claims that his great-grandmother Leona McCurry was part Native American.

PARENTS
Barack Hussein Obama Sr and Stanley Ann Dunham

- Barack Sr was born to Onyango and Akumu in 1936 in Nyangoma-Kogelo, Siaya District, Kenya.
- Ann was born to Stanley and Madelyn on 27 November 1942 in Wichita, Kansas.
- Barack Sr and Ann were married in 1960 in Hawaii and had one child, Barack Obama, President of the United States.
- Obama Sr died in a car crash in Nairobi, Kenya, in

1982, leaving three wives, six sons and a daughter.
- One of his sons died in 1984.
- Obama Sr is buried in the village of Nyangoma-Kogelo, Siaya District, Kenya.
- Ann died of ovarian cancer on 7 November 1995.
- Her ashes were scattered in the Pacific.

GRANDPARENTS
Hussein Onyango Obama
and Akumu

- Onyango was born in 1895 in Kenya.
- Onyango worked for the white oppressors during the period of colonial rule in Kenya, supervising road crews.
- He was 'a prominent farmer, an elder of the tribe, a medicine man with healing powers'.
- He was such a strict disciplinarian that his grandchildren called him 'the Terror'.
- Grandfather Obama was a herbalist who knew how to use plants to heal the sick or wounded – not 'a shaman, what the white man calls a witch doctor', Obama's step-grandmother Sarah Obama is quoted as saying. 'Once he was chased into a tree by an angry buffalo and had to sleep in the tree for two days. Once he found a drum lying in the middle of the forest path and, when he opened it, a snake appeared and slid between his feet into the bush,' according to Sarah.
- He fought for England in World War I, visiting

Europe and India, and afterwards lived for a time in Zanzibar, where he converted from Christianity to Islam.

- Obama's grandfather served as cook for a British officer during World War II.
- He once beat a white employer who tried to cane him.
- He didn't smoke or drink, but he did like to dance. But he was 'not such a good dancer – he was rough, and would bump into people and step on their feet'.
- Hussein Onyango had several wives. His first wife was Helima, with whom he had no children. Akuma was his second wife and they had three children together.
- Little is known about Akumu. The women's 'names are forgotten, for that was the way of our people', as a local was quoted by Barack Jr in his *Dreams from my Father*. A photograph of her holding her son, Barack Sr, on her lap is on the cover of Obama's book.
- Onyango's third wife, Sarah, is the one Barack often refers to as his 'grandmother'. Mama Sarah looked after Barack Obama Sr after his mother, Akuma, left the family when her children were still young.
- Onyango died in 1979 and is buried beside his son in Kogelo in Kenya.

Stanley Armour Dunham
and Madelyn Lee Payne

- Madelyn Lee Payne Dunham was born in Peru, Kansas, on 26 October 1922.

- Her parents were stern Methodists who didn't approve of drinking, playing cards or dancing.

- Madelyn was a bright student and she liked to go to Wichita, Kansas, to see big band concerts, which is where she met Kansas-born Stanley Armour Dunham from the 'other side of the railroad tracks.'

- Barack's grandfather, Stanley Armour Dunham was born on 23 March 1918 in Wichita, Kansas.

- His parents were Baptists.

- When Stanley was eight years old, he discovered his mother's body after she had committed suicide.

- His father abandoned the family and Stanley and his brother, Ralph, were sent to live with his maternal grandparents, Harry and Gabriella Ellington, in El Dorado, Kansas.

- Stanley was kicked out of school for punching the principal.

- He was described as 'gregarious, friendly, impetuous, challenging and loud'.

- Stanley was a furniture salesman and said to be able to 'charm the legs off a couch'.

- Madelyn and Stanley married on 5 May 1940 – the night of Madelyn's senior prom – much to her parents' disapproval.

- Stanley enlisted in the army during World War II

and Madelyn worked on a Boeing B-29 assembly line.

- Madelyn's brother Charlie Payne was part of the 89th Infantry Division, which liberated the Nazi concentration camp at Ohrdruf.
- Madelyn gave birth to Stanley Ann on 29 November 1942.
- The family lived in Berkeley, California, Ponca City, Oklahoma, Vernon, Texas, El Dorado, Kansas, Seattle, Washington and finally settled in Mercer Island, Washington, where Ann graduated from Mercer Island High School.
- Madelyn worked in restaurants along the way.
- Mercer Island was then 'a rural, idyllic place', quiet, politically conservative and all white.
- Madelyn attended the University of Washington though she never completed a degree.
- Madelyn and Stanley then moved to Hawaii, where he found a better furniture store opportunity.
- She started working at the Bank of Hawaii in 1960 and became one of the first female bank vice presidents in 1970.
- Both Dunhams were upset when their daughter married Obama Sr, particularly after receiving a long letter from Obama Sr's father saying he 'didn't want the Obama blood sullied by a white woman'.
- Madelyn was quoted as saying, 'I am a little dubious of the things that people from foreign countries tell me.'

- Barack lived with his grandparents in Hawaii while attending Punahou School.
- As a child, Madelyn read Obama 'the opening lines of the Declaration of Independence and told me about the men and women who marched for equality because they believed those words put to paper two centuries ago should mean something.'
- Obama and his half-sister Maya referred to Madelyn as 'Toot' – short for 'tutu', the Hawaiian word for grandmother.
- She was 'quiet yet firm', compared to Obama's 'boisterous' grandfather Stanley.
- Her colleagues recall her as a 'tough boss' who would make you 'sink or swim', but who had a 'soft spot for those willing to work hard'.
- She retired from the Bank of Hawaii in 1986.
- During Barack's teenage years, Madelyn 'injected' into him 'a lot of that very midwestern, sort of traditional sense of prudence and hard work', even though 'some of those values didn't sort of manifest themselves until I got older'.
- Obama's abiding image of his grandmother is of her coming home from work and trading her business outfit and girdle for a muumuu, some slippers, a drink and a cigarette.
- Stanley Dunham died in Honolulu in 1992 and is buried there in the Punchbowl National Cemetery.
- In later life, Barack's grandmother was an avid bridge player, but mostly she stayed at home

'listening to books on tape and watching her grandson on CNN every day'.

- Madelyn suffered from severe osteoporosis. She underwent a corneal transplant and a hip replacement in 2008.
- When Barack was nominated, she called and said, 'That's nice, Barry, that's nice.'
- According to Barack, his grandmother 'uttered racial or ethnic stereotypes that made me cringe'.
- She appeared briefly in a campaign ad for her grandson, saying that Obama had 'a lot of depth, and a broadness of view'.
- Obama suspended campaign events on 23 and 24 October to spend time with his ailing grandmother. She died on 2 November 2008.
- Barack and his sister Maya released a statement saying, 'She was the cornerstone of our family, and a woman of extraordinary accomplishment, strength, and humility.'
- Her ashes were scattered in the ocean at Lanai Lookout in Hawaii.

GREAT-GRANDPARENTS
Obama and Nyaoke

- Not much is known, except that Obama was born in Kendu Bay, Kenya and had four wives, one of whom was Nyaoke. She fathered many children, of whom Onyango was the fifth son.

Ralph Waldo Emerson Dunham
and Ruth Lucille Armour

- Ralph was born to Jacob and Mary on 24 December 1894 in Argonia, Sumner County, Kansas.
- Ruth was born to Harry and Gabrielle in 1900 in Illinois.
- Ralph and Ruth were married on 3 October 1915 in Wichita, Sedgwick County, Kansas and had two children.
- They opened The Travelers' Cafe on William Street in downtown Wichita, between the old firehouse and the old City Hall.
- Ruth committed suicide on 25 November 1926.
- Ralph died on 4 October 1970 in Wichita.

Rolla Charles Payne
and Leona McCurry

- Rolla was born to Charles and Della on 23 August 1892 in Olathe, Johnson County, Kansas.
- Leona was born to Thomas and Margaret around May 1897 in Kansas.
- Rolla and Leona married in Kansas about 1922 and had three children.
- Rolla died in Kansas in October 1968.

GREAT-GREAT-GRANDPARENTS
Jacob William Dunham
and Mary Ann Kearney

- Jacob was born to Jacob and Louisa on 7 February 1863 in Kempton, Tipton County, Indiana.

- Mary was born to Falmouth and Charlotte on 19 September 1869 in Tipton County, Indiana.
- Jacob and Mary Ann married on 1 March 1890 in Kansas. They lived in Wichita, Sedgwick County, Kansas. They had seven children.
- They both died on 13 August 1936 in Wichita, Sedgwick County, Kansas.

Harry Ellington Armour and Gabriella Clark

- Harry was born to George and Ann on 10 January 1874 in Illinois.
- Gabriella was born to Christopher and Susan about June 1877 in Missouri.
- Harry and Gabriella were married around 1899. They lived in Wichita, Sedgwick County, Kansas and later in El Dorado, Butler County, Kansas.
- The couple had two children.
- Gabriella died on 15 July 1966 in Kansas.

Charles T. Payne and Della Wolfley

- Charles was born to Benjamin and Eliza about June 1861 in Missouri.
- Della was born to Robert and Rachel about May 1863 in Ohio. Her family moved to Kansas just a few years later where she lived out the rest of her life.
- Charles and Della married on 14 January 1889 in Johnson County, Kansas and had six children.

- Della died sometime between 1900 and 1910.
- Charles died sometime after 1930, while he was living with his eldest daughter Lillie in Kansas City.

Thomas Creekmore McCurry and Margaret Belle Wright

- Thomas was born to Harbin and Elizabeth about January 1850 in Ozark County, Missouri.
- Margaret was born to Joseph and Frances on 11 August 1869 in Dry Fork, Carroll County, Arkansas.
- Thomas McCurry was married twice. Margaret was his second wife. They married on 13 March 1885 in Chautauqua County, Kansas. They had seven children.
- Margaret died on 27 November 1935 in Kansas.
- Thomas died in 1939. He is buried next to his wife in Peru Cemetery in Peru.

GREAT-GREAT-GREAT-GRANDPARENTS
Jacob Mackey Dunham and Louisa Eliza Stroup

- Jacob was born on 7 May 1824 in Berkeley County, Virginia (now West Virginia).
- Louisa was born on 8 October 1837 in Madison County, Ohio.
- They had seven children.
- Louisa died on 26 October 1901 in Wellston, Lincoln County, Oklahoma.

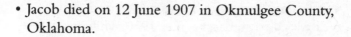
- Jacob died on 12 June 1907 in Okmulgee County, Oklahoma.

Falmouth Kearney and Charlotte Holloway
- Falmouth was born about 1830 in Ireland. He emigrated from Ireland during the Great Irish Famine on the ship *Marmion* on 20 March 1850, along with his sister Margaret Cleary and her husband, William.
- Falmouth lived in Wayne, Fayette County, Ohio, with his aunt and uncle, William and Alice Carney (Kearney), and with his sister Margaret Cleary and her husband William.
- Charlotte was born about 1833 in Ohio.
- Falmouth and Charlotte were married between mid-1850 and 1853 and lived in Deerfield, Ross County, Ohio, next to Charlotte's brother, Joseph Holloway. They then moved to Jefferson, Tipton County, Indiana.
- They had eight children.
- Charlotte died on 11 September 1877.
- Falmouth died on 21 March 1878.

George and Ann Armour
- George was born about 1850 in Ohio.
- Ann was born about 1849 in Missouri.
- George and Ann married around 1872. They lived in Ellington, Adams County, Illinois.
- They had four children.

Christopher Columbus Clark
and Susan C. Overall

- Christopher was born around 1846 in Missouri.
- Susan was born about 1849 in Kentucky.
- Christopher and Susan were married on 6 January 1870 in Nelson County, Kentucky. They lived in Linn, Audrain County, Missouri and in Canton, Lewis County, Missouri.
- They had four children.
- Christopher lived in Ottawa, LaSalle County, Illinois, with his son Joseph after Susan died sometime between 1900 and 1910.
- He then lived with his daughter Gabriella and son-in-law Harry in Wichita, Sedgwick County, Kansas, and finally moved on to El Dorado, Butler County, Kansas.
- Christopher died sometime after 1930.

Benjamin T. Payne
and Eliza C. Black

- Benjamin was born about 1838 in Missouri.
- Eliza was born 3 April 1837 in Quincy, Adams County, Illinois.
- Benjamin and Eliza married sometime before 4 July 1860 in Warren, Marion County, Missouri. They moved to Knox County, Missouri.
- They had two children.
- Benjamin died on 15 April 1878 in Knox County.
- Elisa C. Payne lived in Edina, Knox County, after her husband died.

• She died in 1921 in Kansas City.

Robert Wolfley and Rachel Abbott

• Robert was born about 1835 in Ohio.
• Rachel was born about 1836 in Ohio and died after 1910.
• Robert served in Company A of the 145th Ohio Infantry (National Guard) as a Union soldier during the Civil War.
• Robert and Rachel married on 29 September 1859 in Delaware County, Ohio. They lived in Radnor, Delaware County, Ohio, and in McCamish, Johnson County, Kansas.
• Robert and Rachel had four children.
• Robert died around 1895 in Kansas.
• Rachel applied for a Civil War pension and lived with her youngest son in Olathe, Johnson County, Kansas. She then lived with her oldest daughter, Anna, in Snohomish County, Washington.

Harbin Wilburn McCurry and Elizabeth Edna Creekmore

• Harbin was born on 11 March 1823 in Indiana
• Elizabeth was born on 23 March 1827 in Illinois.
• Harbin and Elizabeth married about 1848 in Missouri. They lived in Ozark County, Missouri, then moved to Newton County and on to Andrew County. By 1875 the family was living in Salt Creek, Howard County, Kansas.

- Harbin and Elizabeth had 11 children.
- Harbin died on 24 July 1899 in Indian Territory (now Oklahoma). He is buried in Center Cemetery in present-day Pontotoc County.
- Elizabeth died on 15 January 1918 in Ada, Pontotoc County, Oklahoma. She is buried in the Rosedale Cemetery in Ada

Joseph J. Wright and Frances Allred

- Joseph was born on 31 July 1819 in Kentucky.
- Frances was born about 1834 in Overton County, Tennessee.
- Joseph was the delegate to the constitutional convention of 1868 from Carroll County, Arkansas.
- Joseph married twice. His first wife was Sarah Obadiah Brown, born about 1818 in North Carolina and died between 1852 and 1855 in Carroll County, Arkansas. They had seven children together.
- Joseph married Frances around 1855 in Tennessee, soon after his first wife's death. They lived in Osage, Carroll County, Arkansas, and later in Dry Fork.
- Frances and Joseph had 12 children.
- Joseph died on 29 April 1894 in Hale, Chautauqua County, Kansas.
- Frances died on 25 May 1918 in Chautauqua County, Kansas.

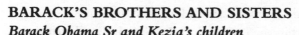

BARACK'S BROTHERS AND SISTERS
Barack Obama Sr and Kezia's children
Abongo Obama

- Abongo, also known as Roy or Malik, was born in March, 1958 in Nairobi.
- He earned a degree in accounting from the University of Nairobi.
- Abongo met half-brother Barack for the first time in 1985. Abongo and his half-brother Barack were best man at each other's weddings.
- Abongo works as a consultant in Washington, DC for several months of the year, and lives in Kogelo, Kenya, for the rest of the time, running a small electronics shop outside the town.
- Abongo was a spokesman for the extended Obama family in Kenya during the presidential campaign.

Auma Obama

- Auma was born in 1960.
- She studied German at the University of Heidelberg from 1981 to 1987. After her graduation in Heidelberg she went on for graduate studies at the University of Bayreuth, which awarded her a PhD in 1996.
- She was a development worker in Kenya.
- Auma lives in London, and in 1996 married Englishman Ian Manners. They have a daughter named Akinyi, who was born in 1997.
- Obama met Auma for the first time after their

father died in a car accident in 1982. In his memoir, Obama recalled that he loved her instantly.

- Auma said, 'Barack was a lot like my father – his hand movements, his gestures, how he talks, how he sits. He's got a certain quietness about him and he sits and he concentrates like my father. He can be in a room full of people and he withdraws on his own. And we've all got the Obama hands – the fingers and everything. So it was amazing to watch that, because I was meeting him for the first time but it felt like I knew him.'

Abo Obama
- Abo Obama was born in 1968.
- He is an international telephone store manager in Kenya.

Bernard Obama
- Bernard Obama was born in 1970.
- Bernard was an auto-parts supplier in Nairobi, Kenya, and has one child.
- He converted to Islam as an adult and has said, 'I'm a Muslim, I don't deny it. My father was raised a Muslim. But it's not an issue. I don't know what all the hullabaloo is about.'
- He lives in Bracknell, England, with his mother Kezia.
- There is a question mark over Barack Sr's paternity, according to Barack's memoirs.

Barack Obama Sr and Ruth Nidesand's children
Mark Ndesandjo

- Mark graduated from Brown University, studied physics at Stanford University, received an MBA from Emory University.
- He is married to a Chinese woman and has lived in Shenzhen, a southern Chinese city bordering Hong Kong, since 2002.
- He came to China as a member of a Sino- American culture exchange programme, and worked in a Shenzhen foreign language school. During this period, he nurtured the idea of establishing a non-profit organisation in China to help orphans.
- He runs an Internet company called WorldNexus that advises Chinese corporations on how to reach international customers.
- He is an accomplished pianist.

David Ndesandjo

- David was also known as David Opiyo Obama.
- He was killed in a motorbike accident in 1984.

Barack Obama Sr and Jael's child
George Hussein Onyango Obama

- George was born in 1982.
- His mother, Jael, is now resident in Atlanta, Georgia.
- He was raised in Nairobi by his mother and a French stepfather.
- He lives on a dollar a month in a Nairobi shantytown.

- He has only met his famous older brother twice –
  once when he was just five and the last time in
  2006 when Senator Obama was on a tour of East
  Africa and visited Nairobi.
- Barack mentions his brother in his autobiography,
  describing him in just one passing paragraph as a
  'beautiful boy with a rounded head'.
- Huruma, where George lives, is a tough place. 'I
  have seen two of my friends killed. I have scars
  from defending myself with my fists. I am good
  with my fists,' says George.

Ann Dunham and Lolo Soetoro
Maya Soetoro-Ng

- Maya was born on 15 August 1970, in Jakarta,
  Indonesia.
- Maya is a Buddhist and holds a PhD in education.
- She is married to Konrad Ng, with whom she has
  a daughter, Suhaila.
- Maya is a teacher in Hawaii.

13

All the
President's Men

❋ Obama's Cabinet is the most ethnically diverse in American history. It includes African-American, Hispanic, Japanese-American, Hawaiian and Chinese-American.

❋ The Cabinet's role is to advise the President on any subject he may require relating to the duties of each member's respective office. It includes the Vice President and the heads of 15 executive departments – the Secretaries of Agriculture, Commerce, Defense, Education, Energy, Health and Human Services, Homeland Security, Housing and Urban Development, Interior, Labor, State, Transportation, Treasury and Veterans Affairs, as well as the Attorney General.

Vice President of the United States
Joseph R. Biden

- Biden became an attorney in 1969, and was elected to a county council in 1970.
- He was a Delaware US Senator from 3 January 1973 until his resignation on 15 January 2009, following his election to the Vice Presidency.
- Biden was the sixth-youngest senator in US history. He was re-elected to the Senate six times, and was the fourth most senior senator at the time of his resignation.
- Joe was a long-time member and former chairman of the Foreign Relations Committee.
- He helped bring about US military assistance and

intervention during the Bosnian War and opposed the Gulf War in 1991.

- He voted in favour of the Iraq War Resolution in 2002, but later proposed resolutions to alter US strategy there.
- He has also served as chairman of the Senate Judiciary Committee, dealing with issues relating to drug policy, crime prevention and civil liberties.
- He was involved in the formation of the Violent Crime Control and Law Enforcement Act and Violence Against Women Act.
- Biden unsuccessfully sought the Democratic presidential nomination in 1988 and 2008, both times dropping out early in the process.
- Biden is the first Roman Catholic and the first Delawarean to become Vice President of the United States.

Department of State Secretary
Hillary Rodham Clinton

- Hillary was born in 1946 and raised in a Chicago suburb where her father owned a textile business.
- She began her political life campaigning for Arizona Republican Barry Goldwater in 1964 before switching parties following the assassinations of Martin Luther King Jr, Robert F. Kennedy and Malcolm X.
- She was student-body President at Wellesley College and appeared in *Life* magazine in 1969 for her widely praised commencement address.

- She met Bill Clinton at law school at Yale. 'If you're going to keep looking at me, and I'm going to keep looking back, we might as well be introduced. I'm Hillary Rodham,' she said.

- She and Bill have one daughter, Chelsea, who was born in 1980.

- Hillary worked as a lawyer and child advocate while Bill was Arkansas Governor; she was Arkansas Woman of the Year in 1983 and Arkansas Young Mother of the Year in 1984; the *National Law Journal* twice named her one of the nation's 100 most influential lawyers.

- She was the first First Lady to set up her own office in the West Wing of the White House, after Bill was elected, and later chaired the failed Task Force on National Health Care.

- She was the first First Lady to win elective office in 2000 when she defeated Rick Lazio to become a New York Senator.

- Hillary's favourite fitness activity, according to her MySpace page, is speed walking. Her hobbies include crossword puzzles, Scrabble and gardening. Organising her closets is stress relief. Sleeping in until 7am is her idea of being naughty.

Department of the Treasury Secretary Timothy F. Geithner

- Geithner was born in New York in 1961, and has lived in East Africa, India, Thailand, China and

Japan. He attended high school at the International School of Bangkok.

- He received a master's in international economics and East Asian studies from Johns Hopkins University.
- He married his school classmate Carole Sonnenfeld Geithner.
- Tim joined the Treasury Department in 1988.
- As President and CEO of the New York Federal Reserve, he oversees the Reserve Bank as it monitors banks in New York, New Jersey, and Fairfield County in Connecticut, extends credit to banks, and conducts foreign exchange market intervention.
- Geithner was directly involved in the move that allowed JP Morgan Chase to acquire Bear Stearns with $29 million provided by the government.
- He would not grant Lehman Brothers the right to become a bank-holding company – a status given to both Morgan Stanley and Goldman Sachs – just days after Lehman filed for bankruptcy.
- According to *The Economist*, he 'snowboards, has tried skateboarding and exudes a sort of hipster-wonkiness, using "way" as a synonym for "very" as in "way consequential"'.
- He also fly-fishes, surfs and plays tennis.

Department of Defense Secretary
Robert M. Gates

- Robert was born in 1943, in Wichita, Kansas, Obama's mother's birthplace.

- He served for 26 years at the CIA, ending his tenure as chief of the spy agency under President George H.W. Bush.
- He was the only entry-level CIA officer ever to end up running the agency.
- From 1974 to 1979, he was on the National Security Council staff at the White House and served there again from 1989 to 1991.

Department of Justice Attorney General
Eric H. Holder Jr

- Holder was born in New York in 1951 to immigrant parents from Barbados.
- He became US Attorney for the District of Columbia in 1993. Four years later, he became Deputy Attorney General. He was the first black person to serve in both positions.
- Holder met Obama in 2004 at a dinner party thrown to welcome the new Senator to Washington. Holder was a fundraiser for Obama during the presidential campaign.
- The day before President George W. Bush was inaugurated, Holder reviewed a pardon application for fugitive billionaire Marc Rich. He was 'neutral leaning toward favourable' on the prospect. Clinton signed the pardon. It was revealed that Rich's wife had donated heavily to Clinton's presidential library.

Department of the Interior Secretary
Kenneth L. Salazar

- Salazar, 53, grew up with seven siblings on a Colorado ranch with no electricity or telephone.
- He sometimes refers to himself as a Mexican-American, though his family has farmed on land that is now New Mexico and Colorado since the 16th century.
- Salazar made his name as a lawyer on water issues. He went on to serve as executive director of Colorado's Department of Natural Resources from 1987 to 1994 and later served as the state's Attorney General from 1999 to 2004.
- He earned a perfect 100 ranking in 2008 from the League of Conservation Voters, a non-partisan organisation that tracks environmental voting records in Congress. His lifetime LCV score is an 81 – the non-partisan LCV Scorecard is the nationally accepted yardstick used to gauge how members of Congress voted on key energy and environmental issues.
- Kenneth made a name for himself by controversially opposing oil-shale leases in the West.

Department of Agriculture Secretary
Thomas J. Vilsack

- Vilsack was abandoned at a Pittsburgh orphanage as a baby and adopted by local parents.
- He has a law degree and became Mayor of Mount

Pleasant, Iowa, in 1987, before going on to serve in the Iowa State Senate from 1992.

- In 1998, he became Governor of Iowa and served two terms.
- Thomas is a strong supporter of biotechnology – he was named Governor of the Year in 2001 by the Biotechnology Industry Organization.
- In 2005, Vilsack signed into law a change that allowed convicted felons to vote after serving their sentences. Some 80,000 ex-cons became eligible to vote.
- Vilsack is an avid runner and ran a marathon in Arkansas in 2005 with the state's then Governor, Republican Mike Huckabee.
- He is in favour of working hard to stop global warming.
- He has never lost an election.
- He has worked as a lawyer in Iowa, been a fellow at the Kennedy School of Government at Harvard and worked for the Iowa State Biosafety Institute.

Department of Commerce Secretary
Gary F. Locke

- Gary Faye Locke was born on 21 January 1950.
- He is a third-generation American with paternal ancestry from Taishan, Guangdong in China.
- Gary's parents gave him the Chinese name 駱家輝 (pronounced Lok Gaa-Fai in Cantonese).
- Locke received the Distinguished Eagle Scout Award from the Boy Scouts of America.

- He has a bachelor's degree and a law degree and is married to Mona Lee, a former television reporter for NBC.
- He served two terms as the 21st Governor of Washington from 1997 to 2005.
- Locke is the first Chinese-American to serve as Governor of a state in United States history.
- Gary was criticised for embracing the Republican Party's no-new-taxes approach to dealing with Washington's budget problems during and after the economic turmoil of 2001.
- Democrats saw Gary Locke as a possible vice-presidential pick. He was chosen to respond to George W. Bush's 2003 State of the Union address.
- In 2003, he announced that he would not seek a third term, saying, 'Despite my deep love of our state, I want to devote more time to my family.'
- The Governor had received hundreds of threatening letters and emails, some threatening to kill his children.
- Locke was co-chairman of Democratic candidate Hillary Clinton's bid for President.

Department of Labor Secretary
Hilda L. Solis

- Hilda was born in 1957. Her mother was a native of Nicaragua and worked on an assembly line. Her father was a Mexican immigrant, and worked as a steward for the Teamsters union.

- Hilda has seven siblings, and was the first in her family to attend university.
- She served in the Office of Hispanic Affairs under the Carter Administration and later in the Office of Management and Budget while earning a master's degree at USC in 1981.
- She reportedly lost 20 pounds while canvassing for her first seat in public office.
- In 1994, she became the first Latina elected to the California State Senate, where she successfully pushed through legislation to increase the minimum wage from $4.25 to $5.75 an hour.
- She was elected to Congress in 2000.
- She became the first woman to win the Profiles in Courage Award from the John F. Kennedy Library Foundation. Solis donated the $25,000 award to local environmental groups.

Department of Health and Human Services Secretary Charles E. Johnson

- Johnson spent 31 years as a public accountant.
- He served as Chief of Staff to the Governor of the State of Utah from 1992 to 1997. He also served as Director of the 2000 re-election campaign for Governor Michael O. Leavitt.
- From 1997 to 2004, Johnson served as a member of the Utah State Board of Regents, which oversees all public institutions of higher education in the state of Utah.

- Charles was Chief Financial Officer of the Environmental Protection Agency.
- Mr Johnson was also President of Huntsman Cancer Foundation from 2001 to 2004.
- Johnson was Assistant Secretary for Budget, Technology, and Finance at the Department of Health and Human Services in 2005 in the Bush administration.

Department of Housing & Urban Development Secretary Shaun L.S. Donovan

- Shaun L.S. Donovan was born in New York in 1966.
- Shaun headed the New York City Department of Housing Preservation and Development.
- He has a master of public administration from the John F. Kennedy School of Government and a master's degree in architecture at the Graduate School of Design.
- Donovan was Deputy Assistant Secretary for Multifamily Housing during the Clinton administration.
- He became New York City's housing commissioner in 2004.
- Donovan worked on the Obama election campaign throughout 2008.

Department of Transportation Secretary Raymond L. LaHood

- LaHood has a wife and four children.

- His grandfather was a Lebanese immigrant.
- His family is Roman Catholic.
- He has degrees in education and sociology, and taught junior high school social studies before entering politics.
- He served in the Illinois House of Representatives from 1982 to 1994, before going on to preside over Bill Clinton's 1998 impeachment trial in the House of Representatives, drawing positive reviews for his handling of the tricky task.
- Raymond spearheaded statewide initiatives to improve transportation and infrastructure, including shoring up local highways and airports.

Department of Energy Secretary Steven Chu

- He was born in St Louis in 1948 to Chinese immigrants who came to America to get their degrees – his father in chemical engineering and his mother in economics.
- Chu grew up on Long Island, New York. His was one of only three Chinese families in his town.
- He is married to a physicist and has two sons from a previous marriage.
- Steven has a PhD in physics from the University of California, Berkeley, where he also taught as a professor.
- He was chair of the Stanford University physics department and head of a research facility at Bell Labs, and is currently director of the Lawrence

Berkeley National Laboratory, which is owned by
the department he is about to lead.
* He is a strong advocate of biofuels and solar energy
research, and is the first Energy secretary who is
also a working scientist.
* He is a Nobel-prize-winning physicist.

Department of Education Secretary
Arne Duncan
* Arne grew up in Hyde Park, Chicago, where his
mother ran a tutoring programme and his father
was a professor at the University of Chicago.
* After graduating with a sociology degree from
Harvard in 1987, Duncan spent four years playing
professional basketball in Australia.
* While in Australia, Duncan also tutored
underprivileged students. He was among the
friends who played basketball with Obama on
Election Day and has played pick-up games
with Michael Jordan.
* Duncan ran the Ariel Education Initiative, a
mentoring and tutoring programme, with his sister
in Chicago. He was head of Chicago schools from
2001, closing failing schools and using
unconventional methods to increase academic
performance.
* Duncan is a strong advocate for performance pay
for teachers and sex-segregated education. He also
supported a proposal for a high school catering to
gay students, called Pride Campus.

- Duncan has offered tickets to sporting events to lure students to school.
- In 2008, Duncan launched a programme in 20 Chicago schools to pay students for good grades. Straight-A students could earn up to $4,000 per year through the programme, funded by private donations.

Department of Veterans Affairs Secretary
Eric K. Shinseki

- Eric was born in Hawaii in 1942 to Japanese-American parents, and is the first Asian-American four-star general in US history.
- He graduated from the United States Military Academy in 1965 and earned an MA in English Literature from Duke University.
- He lost part of his foot during combat in the Vietnam War.
- President Bush, Donald Rumsfeld and Paul Wolfowitz were conspicuously absent from Shinseki's retirement ceremony in 2003.

Department of Homeland Security Secretary
Janet A. Napolitano

- *Time* magazine named Napolitano one of the nation's Top Five Governors in 2005.
- Napolitano was born in New York in 1957 and raised in Albuquerque, New Mexico.
- She is unmarried.
- She has climbed in the Himalayas and reached the

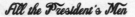

summit of Mount Kilimanjaro.
- Janet loves Monty Python.
- After being appointed by President Bill Clinton, Napolitano served as US Attorney for Arizona and was the first woman to hold the state's Attorney General post.
- She underwent a mastectomy in 2000.
- Napolitano is the first Governor to call for the National Guard to protect the US–Mexico border at federal expense.

Director of the Central Intelligence Agency
Leon Panetta

- Leon was born in Monterey, California, to Catholic Italian immigrant parents who owned a restaurant and later a farm. Panetta worked for both parents' businesses growing up.
- He has a bachelor's degree and a law degree, and served in the army from 1964 to 1966.
- Panetta worked as a Republican aide in the Senate and eventually became head of the US Office for Civil Rights, under President Richard Nixon.
- He was forced to resign after working to desegregate Southern schools.
- Panetta switched to the Democratic Party and returned to California to practise law. He also wrote a book called *Bring Us Together* about his experiences as a civil rights official in the Nixon administration.
- Leon served eight terms in Congress, working on

budgetary matters, environmental causes and civil rights issues.

- He repeatedly voted against President Ronald Reagan's military initiatives.
- He served as Bill Clinton's director of the Office of Management and Budget and was promoted to chief of staff in 1994.
- He was a member of the Iraq Study Group along with Robert Gates before Gates became Defence Secretary.

Council of Economic Advisers Chair Christina Romer

- Christina Romer (née Duckworth) was born in Illinois in 1958.
- She is a Professor of Economics at the University of California, Berkeley.
- She has researched the causes of the Great Depression in the United States and how the US recovered from it.
- Romer, along with Jared Bernstein, wrote the Obama administration's plan for economic recovery.
- Romer found 'no support for the hypothesis that tax cuts restrain government spending; indeed … tax cuts may increase spending'.
- She is married to David Romer, her former classmate at MIT and colleague in the Economics Department; they have adjoining offices and collaborate on much of their research.

- She is a former vice President of the American Economic Association, a John Simon Guggenheim Memorial Foundation Fellowship recipient, a fellow of the American Academy of Arts and Sciences, and a winner of the Berkeley Distinguished Teaching Award.
- Professor Romer is also co-director of the Program in Monetary Economics at the National Bureau of Economic Research.

Environmental Protection Agency Administrator Lisa P. Jackson

- Lisa Perez Jackson was born in Philadelphia in 1962 and adopted weeks after her birth. She grew up in New Orleans and has a master's degree in chemical engineering from Princeton University.
- Jackson began her career at the United States Environmental Protection Agency, where she helped to develop key hazardous waste cleanup regulations, overseeing hazardous waste cleanup projects throughout central New Jersey and directing multimillion-dollar cleanup operations.
- Jackson joined the Department of Environmental Protection (DEP) in March 2002 as assistant commissioner of compliance and enforcement.
- She was a member of Governor of New Jersey Jon S. Corzine's cabinet from 2006 to 2008, serving as Chief of Staff to the Governor and Commissioner of the New Jersey Department of Environmental Protection.

- Lisa is the first African-American to hold this post.

Office of Management & Budget Director
Peter R. Orszag

- Peter Richard Orszag was born in Boston in 1968.
- He has a PhD in economics from the London School of Economics.
- Orszag is divorced and lives in Washington, DC with his two children, Leila and Joshua.
- He was a senior fellow and Deputy Director of Economic Studies at the Brookings Institution, and served as Special Assistant to the President for Economic Policy (1997–98), and as Senior Economist and Senior Adviser on the Council of Economic Advisers (1995–96) during the Clinton administration.
- He runs marathons and enjoys country music.
- During his testimony before the House Budget Committee in March 2009, he said 'there ain't no right way to do the wrong thing', which is a lyric from 'Ain't No Right Way' on Country singer Toby Keith's *White Trash with Money*.
- Before joining the Obama administration, Peter was Director of the Congressional Budget Office.
- At 40, Peter is the youngest member of the Obama Cabinet.

United States Trade Representative
Ronald Kirk

- Ronald Kirk was born in 1954 in Austin, Texas.

- He grew up in a predominantly African-American community.
- He practised law until 1981 when he left to work in the office of then Texas Senator Lloyd Bentsen.
- Kirk was Secretary of State of Texas in 1994.
- In 1995, he became the first African-American Mayor of Dallas, Texas, winning 62 per cent of the vote.
- He was re-elected as Mayor in 1999 with a landslide 74 per cent of the vote.
- In 2001, Kirk resigned as Mayor to run for the Senate, but was unsuccessful.
- Following his defeat, he returned to law and was one of the four highest-paid lobbyists for Energy Future Holdings Corporation.
- Kirk is the first African-American to hold the position of United States Trade Representative.

White House Chief of Staff
Rahm I. Emanuel

- Rahm is married to Amy Rule – a woman he met on a blind date.
- He studied ballet in high school and was offered a scholarship to the Joffrey Ballet, but went to Sarah Lawrence College instead, where he earned a bachelor's degree in Liberal Arts.
- He has a master's degree in speech from Northwestern University.
- Rahm had to have the top of his finger amputated after severing it while slicing meat.

- He worked for Chicago Mayor Richard M. Daley and was first elected to Congress in 2002. He is the fourth-highest-ranking House Democrat.
- Rahm served as a senior adviser to Bill Clinton.
- He is known among colleagues as 'Rahmbo'.
- He has been known to send out cheesecakes to campaign donors and the many Democratic candidates he has recruited over the years.
- Once, when a pollster made Emanuel angry, he sent him a dead fish.
- Emanuel was the basis for Deputy Chief of Staff Josh Lyman, the character played by Bradley Whitford in *The West Wing*.

Press Secretary
Robert Gibbs

- Robert was born in 1971 and is married to attorney Mary Catherine Gibbs. The couple have a six-year old son.
- He studied political science at North Carolina State University, where he was a short-lived goalie for the soccer team.
- Gibbs then worked for several southern congressmen, the Democratic Senatorial Campaign Committee and, briefly, John Kerry's 2004 presidential campaign.
- He has been working for the Obama campaign since 2004.
- Obama wore one of Gibbs's ties during his 2004 Democratic convention speech when the one he

was sporting was deemed unsuitable for TV.
- He shares with the President a love for college football.
- Gibbs has accompanied the Obama family on their summer vacation to Hawaii.

Obama Speaks

Obama's skills as an orator have been compared with Martin Luther King Jr and JFK.

'We, the people, in order to form a more perfect union'
18 March 2008

Two hundred and twenty-one years ago, in a hall that still stands across the street, a group of men gathered and, with these simple words, launched America's improbable experiment in democracy. Farmers and scholars; statesmen and patriots who had travelled across an ocean to escape tyranny and persecution finally made real their declaration of independence at a Philadelphia convention that lasted through the spring of 1787.

The document they produced was eventually signed but ultimately unfinished. It was stained by this nation's original sin of slavery, a question that divided the colonies and brought the convention to a stalemate until the founders chose to allow the slave trade to continue for at least 20 more years, and to leave any final resolution to future generations.

Of course, the answer to the slavery question was already embedded within our Constitution – a Constitution that had at is very core the ideal of equal citizenship under the law; a Constitution that promised its people liberty, and justice, and a union that could be and should be perfected over time.

And yet words on a parchment would not be enough to deliver slaves from bondage, or provide men and women of every colour and creed their full rights and obligations as citizens of the United States. What would be needed were Americans in successive generations who were willing to do their part – through protests and struggle, on the streets and in the courts, through a civil war and civil disobedience and always at great risk – to narrow that gap between the promise of our ideals and the reality of their time.

This was one of the tasks we set forth at the beginning of this campaign – to continue the long march of those who came before us, a march for a more just, more equal, more free, more caring and more prosperous America. I chose to run for the presidency at this moment in history because I believe deeply that we cannot solve the challenges of our time unless we solve them together – unless we perfect our union by understanding that we may have different stories, but we hold common hopes; that we may not look the same and we may not have come from the same place, but we all want to move in the same direction – towards a better future for of children and our grandchildren.

This belief comes from my unyielding faith in the decency and generosity of the American people. But it also comes from my own American story.

I am the son of a black man from Kenya and a white woman from Kansas. I was raised with the help of a white grandfather who survived a Depression to serve in Patton's Army during World War II and a white grandmother who worked on a bomber assembly line at Fort Leavenworth while he was overseas. I've gone to some of the best schools in America and lived in one of the world's poorest nations. I am married to a black American who carries within her the blood of slaves and slaveowners – an inheritance we pass on to our two precious daughters. I have brothers, sisters, nieces, nephews, uncles and cousins, of every race and every hue, scattered across three continents, and, for as long as I live, I will never forget that in no other country on Earth is my story even possible.

It's a story that hasn't made me the most conventional candidate. But it is a story that has seared into my genetic makeup the idea that this nation is more than the sum of its parts – that out of many, we are truly one.

Throughout the first year of this campaign,

against all predictions to the contrary, we saw how hungry the American people were for this message of unity. Despite the temptation to view my candidacy through a purely racial lens, we won commanding victories in states with some of the whitest populations in the country. In South Carolina, where the Confederate Flag still flies, we built a powerful coalition of African-Americans and white Americans.

This is not to say that race has not been an issue in the campaign. At various stages in the campaign, some commentators have deemed me either 'too black' or 'not black enough'. We saw racial tensions bubble to the surface during the week before the South Carolina primary. The press has scoured every exit poll for the latest evidence of racial polarisation, not just in terms of white and black, but black and brown as well.

And yet, it has only been in the last couple of weeks that the discussion of race in this campaign has taken a particularly divisive turn.

On one end of the spectrum, we've heard the implication that my candidacy is somehow an exercise in affirmative action; that it's based solely on the desire of wide-eyed liberals to purchase racial reconciliation on the cheap. On the other end, we've heard my former pastor, Reverend Jeremiah Wright, use incendiary language to

express views that have the potential not only to widen the racial divide, but views that denigrate both the greatness and the goodness of our nation; that rightly offend white and black alike.

I have already condemned, in unequivocal terms, the statements of Reverend Wright that have caused such controversy. For some, nagging questions remain. Did I know him to be an occasionally fierce critic of American domestic and foreign policy? Of course. Did I ever hear him make remarks that could be considered controversial while I sat in church? Yes. Did I strongly disagree with many of his political views? Absolutely – just as I'm sure many of you have heard remarks from your pastors, priests, or rabbis with which you strongly disagreed.

But the remarks that have caused this recent firestorm weren't simply controversial. They weren't simply a religious leader's effort to speak out against perceived injustice. Instead, they expressed a profoundly distorted view of this country – a view that sees white racism as endemic, and that elevates what is wrong with America above all that we know is right with America; a view that sees the conflicts in the Middle East as rooted primarily in the actions of stalwart allies like Israel, instead of emanating from the perverse and hateful ideologies of radical Islam.

As such, Reverend Wright's comments were not only wrong but divisive, divisive at a time when we need unity; racially charged at a time when we need to come together to solve a set of monumental problems — two wars, a terrorist threat, a falling economy, a chronic healthcare crisis and potentially devastating climate change; problems that are neither black or white or Latino or Asian, but rather problems that confront us all.

Given my background, my politics, and my professed values and ideals, there will no doubt be those for whom my statements of condemnation are not enough. Why associate myself with Reverend Wright in the first place? they may ask. Why not join another church? And I confess that, if all that I knew of Reverend Wright were the snippets of those sermons that have run in an endless loop on the television and YouTube, or if Trinity United Church of Christ conformed to the caricatures being peddled by some commentators, there is no doubt that I would react in much the same way

But the truth is, that isn't all that I know of the man. The man I met more than 20 years ago is a man who helped introduce me to my Christian faith, a man who spoke to me about our obligations to love one another; to care for the sick and lift up the poor. He is a man who served his country as a US Marine; who has studied and lectured at some of the finest universities and seminaries in the country, and who for over 30 years led a church that serves the community by doing God's work here on Earth – by housing the homeless, ministering to the needy, providing day care services and scholarships and prison ministries, and reaching out to those suffering from HIV/AIDS.

In my first book, *Dreams from My Father*, I described the experience of my first service at Trinity:

'People began to shout, to rise from their seats and clap and cry out, a forceful wind carrying the reverend's voice up into the rafters ... And in that single note – hope! – I heard something else; at the foot of that cross, inside the thousands of churches across the city, I imagined the stories of ordinary black people merging with the stories of David and Goliath, Moses and Pharaoh, the Christians in the lion's den, Ezekiel's field of dry bones. Those stories – of survival, and freedom, and hope – became our story, my story; the blood that had spilled was our blood, the tears our tears; until this black church, on this bright day, seemed once more a vessel carrying the story of a people into future generations and into a larger world.

Our trials and triumphs became at once unique and universal, black and more than black; in chronicling our journey, the stories and songs gave us a means to reclaim memories that we didn't need to feel shame about ... memories that all people might study and cherish – and with which we could start to rebuild.'

That has been my experience at Trinity. Like other predominantly black churches across the country, Trinity embodies the black community in its entirety – the doctor and the welfare mom, the model student and the former gang-banger. Like other black churches, Trinity's services are full of raucous laughter and sometimes bawdy humour. They are full of dancing, clapping, screaming and shouting that may seem jarring to the untrained ear. The church contains in full the kindness and cruelty, the fierce intelligence and the shocking ignorance, the struggles and successes, the love and, yes, the bitterness and bias that make up the black experience in America.

And this helps explain, perhaps, my relationship with Reverend Wright. As imperfect as he may be, he has been like family to me. He strengthened my faith, officiated my wedding, and baptised my children. Not once in my conversations with him have I heard him talk about any ethnic group in derogatory terms, or treat whites with whom he interacted with anything but courtesy and respect. He contains within him the contradictions – the good and the bad – of the community that he has served diligently for so many years.

I can no more disown him than I can disown the black community. I can no more disown him than I can my white grandmother – a woman who helped raise me, a woman who sacrificed again and again for me, a woman who loves me as much as she loves anything in this world, but a woman who once confessed her fear of black men who passed by her on the street, and who on more than one occasion has uttered racial or ethnic stereotypes that made me cringe.

These people are a part of me. And they are a part of America, this country that I love.

Some will see this as an attempt to justify or excuse comments that are simply inexcusable. I can assure you it is not. I suppose the politically safe thing would be to move on from this episode and just hope that it fades into the woodwork. We can dismiss Reverend Wright as a crank or a demagogue, just as some have dismissed Geraldine Ferraro, in the aftermath of her recent statements, as harbouring some deep-seated racial bias.

But race is an issue that I believe this nation

cannot afford to ignore right now. We would be making the same mistake that Reverend Wright made in his offending sermons about America — to simplify and stereotype and amplify the negative to the point that it distorts reality.

The fact is that the comments that have been made and the issues that have surfaced over the last few weeks reflect the complexities of race in this country that we've never really worked through — a part of our union that we have yet to perfect. And if we walk away now, if we simply retreat into our respective corners, we will never be able to come together and solve challenges like healthcare, or education, or the need to find good jobs for every American.

Understanding this reality requires a reminder of how we arrived at this point. As William Faulkner once wrote, 'The past isn't dead and buried. In fact, it isn't even past.' We do not need to recite here the history of racial injustice in this country. But we do need to remind ourselves that so many of the disparities that exist in the African-American community today can be directly traced to inequalities passed on from an earlier generation that suffered under the brutal legacy of slavery and Jim Crow.

Segregated schools were, and are, inferior schools; we still haven't fixed them, 50 years after

Brown v. Board of Education, and the inferior education they provided, then and now, helps explain the pervasive achievement gap between today's black and white students.

Legalised discrimination – where blacks were prevented, often through violence, from owning property, or loans were not granted to African-American business owners, or black homeowners could not access FHA mortgages, or blacks were excluded from unions, or the police force, or fire departments – meant that black families could not amass any meaningful wealth to bequeath to future generations. That history helps explain the wealth and income gap between black and white, and the concentrated pockets of poverty that persists in so many of today's urban and rural communities.

A lack of economic opportunity among black men, and the shame and frustration that came from not being able to provide for one's family, contributed to the erosion of black families – a problem that welfare policies for many years may have worsened. And the lack of basic services in so many urban black neighbourhoods – parks for kids to play in, police walking the beat, regular garbage pick-up and building code enforcement – all helped create a cycle of violence, blight and neglect that continue to haunt us.

This is the reality in which Reverend Wright

and other African-Americans of his generation grew up. They came of age in the late fifties and early sixties, a time when segregation was still the law of the land and opportunity was systematically constricted. What's remarkable is not how many failed in the face of discrimination, but rather how many men and women overcame the odds; how many were able to make a way out of no way for those like me who would come after them.

But for all those who scratched and clawed their way to get a piece of the American Dream, there were many who didn't make it — those who were ultimately defeated, in one way or another, by discrimination. That legacy of defeat was passed on to future generations — those young men and increasingly young women who we see standing on street corners or languishing in our prisons, without hope or prospects for the future. Even for those blacks who did make it, questions of race, and racism, continue to define their worldview in fundamental ways. For the men and women of Reverend Wright's generation, the memories of humiliation and doubt and fear have not gone away; nor has the anger and the bitterness of those years. That anger may not get expressed in public, in front of white co-workers or white friends. But it does find voice in the barbershop or around the kitchen table. At times, that anger is exploited by politicians, to gin up votes along racial lines, or to make up for a politician's own failings.

And occasionally it finds voice in the church on Sunday morning, in the pulpit and in the pews. The fact that so many people are surprised to hear that anger in some of Reverend Wright's sermons simply reminds us of the old truism that the most segregated hour in American life occurs on Sunday morning. That anger is not always productive; indeed, all too often it distracts attention from solving real problems; it keeps us from squarely facing our own complicity in our condition, and prevents the African-American community from forging the alliances it needs to bring about real change. But the anger is real; it is powerful; and to simply wish it away, to condemn it without understanding its roots, only serves to widen the chasm of misunderstanding that exists between the races.

In fact, a similar anger exists within segments of the white community. Most working- and middle-class white Americans don't feel that they have been particularly privileged by their race. Their experience is the immigrant experience – as far as they're concerned, no one's handed them anything, they've built it from scratch. They've worked hard all their lives, many times only to see their jobs shipped overseas or their pension dumped after a lifetime of labour. They are anxious about their futures, and feel their dreams slipping away; in an era of stagnant wages and global competition, opportunity comes to be seen as a zero sum game, in which your dreams come at my expense. So when they are told to bus their children to a school across town; when they hear that an African-American is getting an advantage in landing a good job or a spot in a good college because of an injustice that they themselves never committed; when they're told that their fears about crime in urban neighbourhoods are somehow prejudiced, resentment builds over time.

Like the anger within the black community, these resentments aren't always expressed in polite company. But they have helped shape the political landscape for at least a generation. Anger over welfare and affirmative action helped forge the Reagan Coalition. Politicians routinely exploited fears of crime for their own electoral ends. Talk-show hosts and conservative commentators built entire careers unmasking bogus claims of racism while dismissing legitimate discussions of racial injustice and inequality as mere political correctness or reverse racism.

Just as black anger often proved counterproductive, so have these white resentments distracted attention from the real culprits of the middle-class squeeze — a corporate culture rife with inside dealing, questionable accounting practices and short-term greed; a Washington dominated by lobbyists and special interests; economic policies that favour the few over the many. And yet, to wish away the resentments of white Americans, to label them as misguided or even racist, without recognising they are grounded in legitimate concerns — this too widens the racial divide, and blocks the path to understanding.

This is where we are right now. It's a racial stalemate we've been stuck in for years. Contrary to the claims of some of my critics, black and white, I have never been so naïve as to believe that we can get beyond our racial divisions in a single election cycle, or with a single candidacy — particularly a candidacy as imperfect as my own.

But I have asserted a firm conviction — a conviction rooted in my faith in God and my faith in the American people — that working together we can move beyond some of our old racial wounds, and that, in fact, we have no choice if we are to continue on the path of a more perfect union.

For the African-American community, that path means embracing the burdens of our past without becoming victims of our past. It means continuing to insist on a full measure of justice in every aspect of American life. But it also means binding our particular grievances – for better healthcare, and better schools, and better jobs – to the larger aspirations of all Americans — the white woman struggling to break the glass ceiling, the white man who's been laid off, the immigrant trying to feed his family. And it means taking full responsibility for our own lives – by demanding more from our fathers, and spending more time with our children, and reading to them, and teaching them that, while they may face challenges and discrimination in their own lives, they must never succumb to despair or cynicism; they must always believe that they can write their own destiny.

Ironically, this quintessentially American – and yes, conservative – notion of self-help found frequent expression in Reverend Wright's sermons. But what my former pastor too often failed to understand is that embarking on a programme of self-help also requires a belief that society can change.

The profound mistake of Reverend Wright's sermons is not that he spoke about racism in our society. It's that he spoke as if our society was static; as if no progress has been made; as if this country – a country that has made it possible for one of his own members to run for the highest office in the land and build a coalition of white and black; Latino and Asian, rich and poor, young and old — is still irrevocably bound to a tragic past. But what we know — what we have seen — is that America can change. That is true genius of this nation. What we have already achieved gives us hope — the audacity to hope — for what we can and must achieve tomorrow.

In the white community, the path to a more perfect union means acknowledging that what ails the African-American community does not just exist in the minds of black people; that the legacy of discrimination and current incidents of discrimination — while less overt than in the past — are real and must be addressed. Not just with words, but with deeds — by investing in our schools and our communities; by enforcing our civil-rights laws and ensuring fairness in our criminal justice system; by providing this generation with ladders of opportunity that were unavailable for previous generations. It requires all Americans to realise that your dreams do not have to come at the expense of my dreams; that investing in the health, welfare and education of black and brown and white children will ultimately help all of America prosper.

In the end, then, what is called for is nothing more, and nothing less, than what all the world's great religions demand – that we do unto others as we would have them do unto us. Let us be our brother's keeper, Scripture tells us. Let us be our sister's keeper. Let us find that common stake we all have in one another, and let our politics reflect that spirit as well.

For we have a choice in this country. We can accept a politics that breeds division, and conflict, and cynicism. We can tackle race only as spectacle – as we did in the OJ trial – or in the wake of tragedy, as we did in the aftermath of Katrina – or as fodder for the nightly news. We can play Reverend Wright's sermons on every channel, every day and talk about them from now until the election, and make the only question in this campaign whether or not the American people think that I somehow believe or sympathise with his most offensive words. We can pounce on some gaffe by a Hillary supporter as evidence that she's playing the race card, or we can speculate on whether white men will all flock to John McCain in the general election regardless of his policies.

We can do that.

But, if we do, I can tell you that, in the next election, we'll be talking about some other distraction. And then another one. And then another one. And nothing will change.

That is one option. Or, at this moment, in this

election, we can come together and say, 'Not this time.' This time we want to talk about the crumbling schools that are stealing the future of black children and white children and Asian children and Hispanic children and Native American children. This time we want to reject the cynicism that tells us that these kids can't learn; that those kids who don't look like us are somebody else's problem. The children of America are not those kids, they are our kids, and we will not let them fall behind in a 21st-century economy. Not this time.

This time we want to talk about how the lines in the emergency room are filled with whites and blacks and Hispanics who do not have healthcare; who don't have the power on their own to overcome the special interests in Washington, but who can take them on if we do it together.

This time we want to talk about the shuttered mills that once provided a decent life for men and women of every race, and the homes for sale that once belonged to Americans from every religion, every region, every walk of life. This time we want to talk about the fact that the real problem is not that someone who doesn't look like you might take your job; it's that the corporation you work for will ship it overseas for nothing more than a profit.

This time we want to talk about the men and women of every colour and creed who serve together, and fight together, and bleed together under the same proud flag. We want to talk about how to bring them home from a war that never should've been authorised and never should've been waged, and we want to talk about how we'll show our patriotism by caring for them, and their families, and giving them the benefits they have earned.

I would not be running for President if I didn't believe with all my heart that this is what the vast majority of Americans want for this country. This union may never be perfect, but generation after generation has shown that it can always be perfected. And today, whenever I find myself feeling doubtful or cynical about this possibility, what gives me the most hope is the next generation – the young people whose attitudes and beliefs and openness to change have already made history in this election.

There is one story in particular that I'd like to leave you with today – a story I told when I had the great honour of speaking on Dr King's birthday at his home church, Ebenezer Baptist, in Atlanta.

There is a young, 23-year-old white woman named Ashley Baia who organised for our campaign in Florence, South Carolina. She had been working to organise a mostly African-American community since the beginning of this campaign, and one day she was at a roundtable discussion where everyone went around telling their story and why they were there.

And Ashley said that, when she was nine years old, her mother got cancer. And because she had to miss days of work, she was let go and lost her healthcare. They had to file for bankruptcy, and that's when Ashley decided that she had to do something to help her mom.

She knew that food was one of their most expensive costs, and so Ashley convinced her mother that what she really liked and really wanted to eat more than anything else was mustard and relish sandwiches. Because that was the cheapest way to eat.

She did this for a year until her mom got better, and she told everyone at the roundtable that the reason she joined our campaign was so that she could help the millions of other children in the country who want and need to help their parents too.

Now Ashley might have made a different choice. Perhaps somebody told her along the way that the source of her mother's problems were blacks who were on welfare and too lazy to work,

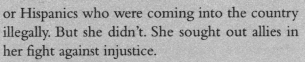

or Hispanics who were coming into the country illegally. But she didn't. She sought out allies in her fight against injustice.

Anyway, Ashley finishes her story and then goes around the room and asks everyone else why they're supporting the campaign. They all have different stories and reasons. Many bring up a specific issue. And finally they come to this elderly black man who's been sitting there quietly the entire time. And Ashley asks him why he's there. And he does not bring up a specific issue. He does not say healthcare or the economy. He does not say education or the war. He does not say that he was there because of Barack Obama. He simply says to everyone in the room, 'I am here because of Ashley.'

'I'm here because of Ashley.' By itself, that single moment of recognition between that young white girl and that old black man is not enough. It is not enough to give healthcare to the sick, or jobs to the jobless, or education to our children.

But it is where we start. It is where our union grows stronger. And as so many generations have come to realise over the course of the two hundred and twenty-one years since a band of patriots signed that document in Philadelphia, that is where the perfection begins.

The American Promise Acceptance Speech at the Democratic Convention Mile High Stadium, Denver, Colorado
28 August 2008

To Chairman Dean and my great friend Dick Durbin; and to all my fellow citizens of this great nation;

With profound gratitude and great humility, I accept your nomination for the presidency of the United States.

Let me express my thanks to the historic slate of candidates who accompanied me on this journey, and especially the one who travelled the farthest – a champion for working Americans and an inspiration to my daughters and to yours — Hillary Rodham Clinton. To President Clinton, who last night made the case for change as only he can make it; to Ted Kennedy, who embodies the spirit of service; and to the next Vice President of the United States, Joe Biden, I thank you. I am grateful to finish this journey with one of the finest statesmen of our time, a man at ease with everyone from world leaders to the conductors on the Amtrak train he still takes home every night.

To the love of my life, our next First Lady, Michelle Obama, and to Sasha and Malia – I love you so much, and I'm so proud of all of you.

Four years ago, I stood before you and told you my story – of the brief union between a young man from Kenya and a young woman from Kansas who weren't well off or well known, but shared a belief that, in America, their son could achieve whatever he put his mind to.

It is that promise that has always set this country apart – that, through hard work and sacrifice, each of us can pursue our individual dreams but still come together as one American family, to ensure that the next generation can pursue their dreams as well.

That's why I stand here tonight. Because for 232 years, at each moment when that promise was in jeopardy, ordinary men and women – students and soldiers, farmers and teachers, nurses and janitors – found the courage to keep it alive.

We meet at one of those defining moments – a moment when our nation is at war, our economy is in turmoil, and the American promise has been threatened once more.

Tonight, more Americans are out of work and more are working harder for less. More of you have lost your homes and even more are watching your home values plummet. More of you have cars you can't afford to drive, credit-card bills you can't afford to pay, and tuition that's beyond your reach.

These challenges are not all of government's making. But the failure to respond is a direct result of a broken politics in Washington and the failed policies of George W. Bush.

America, we are better than these last eight years. We are a better country than this.

This country is more decent than one where a woman in Ohio, on the brink of retirement, finds herself one illness away from disaster after a lifetime of hard work.

This country is more generous than one where a man in Indiana has to pack up the equipment he's worked on for 20 years and watch it shipped off to China, and then chokes up as he explains how he felt like a failure when he went home to tell his family the news.

We are more compassionate than a government that lets veterans sleep on our streets and families slide into poverty; that sits on its hands while a major American city drowns before our eyes.

Tonight, I say to the American people, to Democrats and Republicans and Independents across this great land – enough! This moment – this election – is our chance to keep, in the 21st century, the American promise alive. Because next

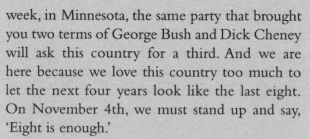

week, in Minnesota, the same party that brought you two terms of George Bush and Dick Cheney will ask this country for a third. And we are here because we love this country too much to let the next four years look like the last eight. On November 4th, we must stand up and say, 'Eight is enough.'

Now let there be no doubt. The Republican nominee, John McCain, has worn the uniform of our country with bravery and distinction, and for that we owe him our gratitude and respect. And next week, we'll also hear about those occasions when he's broken with his party as evidence that he can deliver the change that we need.

But the record's clear: John McCain has voted with George Bush 90 per cent of the time. Senator McCain likes to talk about judgement, but really, what does it say about your judgement when you think George Bush has been right more than 90 per cent of the time? I don't know about you, but I'm not ready to take a 10 per cent chance on change.

The truth is, on issue after issue that would make a difference in your lives – on healthcare and education and the economy – Senator McCain has been anything but independent. He said that our economy has made 'great progress' under this President. He said that the fundamentals of the

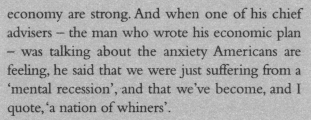

economy are strong. And when one of his chief advisers – the man who wrote his economic plan – was talking about the anxiety Americans are feeling, he said that we were just suffering from a 'mental recession', and that we've become, and I quote, 'a nation of whiners'.

A nation of whiners? Tell that to the proud auto workers at a Michigan plant who, after they found out it was closing, kept showing up every day and working as hard as ever, because they knew there were people who counted on the brakes that they made. Tell that to the military families who shoulder their burdens silently as they watch their loved ones leave for their third or fourth or fifth tour of duty. These are not whiners. They work hard and give back and keep going without complaint. These are the Americans that I know.

Now, I don't believe that Senator McCain doesn't care what's going on in the lives of Americans. I just think he doesn't know. Why else would he define middle-class as someone making under five million dollars a year? How else could he propose hundreds of billions in tax breaks for big corporations and oil companies but not one penny of tax relief to more than one hundred million Americans? How else could he offer a healthcare plan that would actually tax people's benefits, or an education plan that would do nothing to help families pay for college, or a plan that would privatise Social Security and gamble your retirement?

It's not because John McCain doesn't care. It's because John McCain doesn't get it.

For over two decades, he's subscribed to that old, discredited Republican philosophy — give more and more to those with the most and hope that prosperity trickles down to everyone else. In Washington, they call this the Ownership Society, but what it really means is — you're on your own. Out of work? Tough luck. No healthcare? The market will fix it. Born into poverty? Pull yourself up by your own bootstraps — even if you don't have boots. You're on your own.

Well, it's time for them to own their failure. It's time for us to change America.

You see, we Democrats have a very different measure of what constitutes progress in this country.

We measure progress by how many people can find a job that pays the mortgage; whether you can put a little extra money away at the end of each month so you can someday watch your child receive her college diploma. We measure progress in the 23 million new jobs that were created when Bill Clinton was President — when the average American family saw its income go up $7,500 instead of down $2,000 like it has under George Bush.

We measure the strength of our economy not by the number of billionaires we have or the profits of the Fortune 500, but by whether someone with a good idea can take a risk and start a new business, or whether the waitress who lives on tips can take a day off to look after a sick kid without losing her job – an economy that honours the dignity of work.

The fundamentals we use to measure economic strength are whether we are living up to that fundamental promise that has made this country great – a promise that is the only reason I am standing here tonight.

Because in the faces of those young veterans who come back from Iraq and Afghanistan, I see my grandfather, who signed up after Pearl Harbor, marched in Patton's Army, and was rewarded by a grateful nation with the chance to go to college on the GI Bill.

In the face of that young student who sleeps just three hours before working the night shift, I think about my mom, who raised my sister and me on her own while she worked and earned her degree; who once turned to food stamps but was still able to send us to the best schools in the country with the help of student loans and scholarships.

When I listen to another worker tell me that his factory has shut down, I remember all those men and women on the South Side of Chicago who I stood by and fought for two decades ago after the local steel plant closed.

And when I hear a woman talk about the difficulties of starting her own business, I think about my grandmother, who worked her way up from the secretarial pool to middle-management, despite years of being passed over for promotions because she was a woman. She's the one who taught me about hard work. She's the one who put off buying a new car or a new dress for herself so that I could have a better life. She poured everything she had into me. And, although she can no longer travel, I know that she's watching tonight, and that tonight is her night as well.

I don't know what kind of lives John McCain thinks that celebrities lead, but this has been mine. These are my heroes. Theirs are the stories that shaped me. And it is on their behalf that I intend to win this election and keep our promise alive as President of the United States.

What is that promise?

It's a promise that says each of us has the

freedom to make of our own lives what we will, but that we also have the obligation to treat each other with dignity and respect.

It's a promise that says the market should reward drive and innovation and generate growth, but that businesses should live up to their responsibilities to create American jobs, look out for American workers and play by the rules of the road.

Ours is a promise that says government cannot solve all our problems, but what it should do is that which we cannot do for ourselves – protect us from harm and provide every child a decent education; keep our water clean and our toys safe; invest in new schools and new roads and new science and technology.

Our government should work for us, not against us. It should help us, not hurt us. It should ensure opportunity not just for those with the most money and influence, but for every American who's willing to work.

That's the promise of America – the idea that we are responsible for ourselves, but that we also rise or fall as one nation; the fundamental belief that I am my brother's keeper; I am my sister's keeper.

That's the promise we need to keep. That's the change we need right now. So let me spell out exactly what that change would mean if I am President.

Change means a tax code that doesn't reward the lobbyists who wrote it, but the American workers and small businesses who deserve it.

Unlike John McCain, I will stop giving tax breaks to corporations that ship jobs overseas, and I will start giving them to companies that create good jobs right here in America.

I will eliminate capital gains taxes for the small businesses and the start-ups that will create the high-wage, high-tech jobs of tomorrow.

I will cut taxes – cut taxes – for 95 per cent of all working families. Because in an economy like this, the last thing we should do is raise taxes on the middle class.

And for the sake of our economy, our security, and the future of our planet, I will set a clear goal as President: in ten years, we will finally end our dependence on oil from the Middle East.

Washington's been talking about our oil addiction for the last 30 years, and John McCain has been there for 26 of them. In that time, he's said no to higher fuel-efficiency standards for cars, no to investments in renewable energy, no to renewable fuels. And today, we import triple the amount of oil as the day that Senator McCain took office.

Now is the time to end this addiction, and to understand that drilling is a stop–gap measure, not a long-term solution. Not even close.

As President, I will tap our natural gas reserves, invest in clean coal technology, and find ways to safely harness nuclear power. I'll help our auto companies re-tool, so that the fuel-efficient cars of the future are built right here in America. I'll make it easier for the American people to afford these new cars. And I'll invest $150 billion over the next decade in affordable, renewable sources of energy – wind power and solar power and the next generation of biofuels; an investment that will lead to new industries and five million new jobs that pay well and can't ever be outsourced.

America, now is not the time for small plans.

Now is the time to finally meet our moral obligation to provide every child a world-class education, because it will take nothing less to compete in the global economy. Michelle and I are only here tonight because we were given a chance at an education. And I will not settle for an America where some kids don't have that chance. I'll invest in early childhood education. I'll recruit an army of new teachers, and pay them higher salaries and give them more support. And, in exchange, I'll ask for higher standards and more accountability. And we will keep our promise to

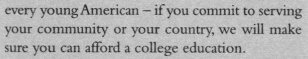

every young American – if you commit to serving your community or your country, we will make sure you can afford a college education.

Now is the time to finally keep the promise of affordable, accessible healthcare for every single American. If you have healthcare, my plan will lower your premiums. If you don't, you'll be able to get the same kind of coverage that members of Congress give themselves. And as someone who watched my mother argue with insurance companies while she lay in bed dying of cancer, I will make certain those companies stop discriminating against those who are sick and need care the most.

Now is the time to help families with paid sick days and better family leave, because nobody in America should have to choose between keeping their jobs and caring for a sick child or ailing parent.

Now is the time to change our bankruptcy laws, so that your pensions are protected ahead of CEO bonuses; and the time to protect Social Security for future generations.

And now is the time to keep the promise of equal pay for an equal day's work, because I want my daughters to have exactly the same opportunities as your sons.

Now, many of these plans will cost money,

which is why I've laid out how I'll pay for every dime — by closing corporate loopholes and tax havens that don't help America grow. But I will also go through the federal budget, line by line, eliminating programmes that no longer work and making the ones we do need work better and cost less — because we cannot meet 21st-century challenges with a 20th-century bureaucracy.

And Democrats, we must also admit that fulfilling America's promise will require more than just money. It will require a renewed sense of responsibility from each of us to recover what John F. Kennedy called our 'intellectual and moral strength'. Yes, government must lead on energy independence, but each of us must do our part to make our homes and businesses more efficient. Yes, we must provide more ladders to success for young men who fall into lives of crime and despair. But we must also admit that programmes alone can't replace parents; that government can't turn off the television and make a child do her homework; that fathers must take more responsibility for providing the love and guidance their children need.

Individual responsibility and mutual responsibility — that's the essence of America's promise.

And just as we keep our promise to the next generation here at home, so must we keep

America's promise abroad. If John McCain wants to have a debate about who has the temperament, and judgement, to serve as the next Commander-in-Chief, that's a debate I'm ready to have.

For while Senator McCain was turning his sights to Iraq just days after 9/11, I stood up and opposed this war, knowing that it would distract us from the real threats we face. When John McCain said we could just 'muddle through' in Afghanistan, I argued for more resources and more troops to finish the fight against the terrorists who actually attacked us on 9/11, and made clear that we must take out Osama bin Laden and his lieutenants if we have them in our sights. John McCain likes to say that he'll follow bin Laden to the Gates of Hell – but he won't even go to the cave where he lives.

And today, as my call for a timeframe to remove our troops from Iraq has been echoed by the Iraqi government and even the Bush administration, even after we learned that Iraq has a $79 billion surplus while we're wallowing in deficits, John McCain stands alone in his stubborn refusal to end a misguided war.

That's not the judgement we need. That won't keep America safe. We need a President who can face the threats of the future, not keep grasping at the ideas of the past.

You don't defeat a terrorist network that operates in 80 countries by occupying Iraq. You don't protect Israel and deter Iran just by talking tough in Washington. You can't truly stand up for Georgia when you've strained our oldest alliances. If John McCain wants to follow George Bush with more tough talk and bad strategy, that is his choice – but it is not the change we need.

We are the party of Roosevelt. We are the party of Kennedy. So don't tell me that Democrats won't defend this country. Don't tell me that Democrats won't keep us safe. The Bush–McCain foreign policy has squandered the legacy that generations of Americans – Democrats and Republicans – have built, and we are here to restore that legacy.

As Commander-in-Chief, I will never hesitate to defend this nation, but I will only send our troops into harm's way with a clear mission and a sacred commitment to give them the equipment they need in battle and the care and benefits they deserve when they come home.

I will end this war in Iraq responsibly, and finish the fight against al Qaeda and the Taliban in Afghanistan. I will rebuild our military to meet future conflicts. But I will also renew the tough, direct diplomacy that can prevent Iran from obtaining nuclear weapons and curb Russian aggression. I will build new partnerships to defeat the threats of the 21st century: terrorism and nuclear proliferation; poverty and genocide; climate change and disease. And I will restore our moral standing, so that America is once again that last, best hope for all who are called to the cause of freedom, who long for lives of peace, and who yearn for a better future.

These are the policies I will pursue. And in the weeks ahead, I look forward to debating them with John McCain.

But what I will not do is suggest that the Senator takes his positions for political purposes. Because one of the things that we have to change in our politics is the idea that people cannot disagree without challenging each other's character and patriotism.

The times are too serious, the stakes are too high for this same partisan playbook. So let us agree that patriotism has no party. I love this country, and so do you, and so does John McCain. The men and women who serve in our battlefields may be Democrats and Republicans and Independents, but they have fought together and bled together and some died together under the same proud flag. They have not served a Red America or a Blue America – they have served the United States of America.

So I've got news for you, John McCain. We all put our country first.

America, our work will not be easy. The challenges we face require tough choices, and Democrats as well as Republicans will need to cast off the worn-out ideas and politics of the past. For part of what has been lost these past eight years can't just be measured by lost wages or bigger trade deficits. What has also been lost is our sense of common purpose – our sense of higher purpose. And that's what we have to restore.

We may not agree on abortion, but surely we can agree on reducing the number of unwanted pregnancies in this country. The reality of gun ownership may be different for hunters in rural Ohio than for those plagued by gang-violence in Cleveland, but don't tell me we can't uphold the Second Amendment while keeping AK-47s out of the hands of criminals. I know there are differences on same-sex marriage, but surely we can agree that our gay and lesbian brothers and sisters deserve to visit the person they love in the hospital and to live lives free of discrimination. Passions fly on immigration, but I don't know anyone who benefits when a mother is separated from her infant child or an employer undercuts American wages by hiring illegal workers. This too is part of America's promise – the promise of a democracy where we can find the strength and grace to bridge divides and unite in common effort.

I know there are those who dismiss such beliefs as happy talk. They claim that our insistence on something larger, something firmer and more honest in our public life is just a Trojan Horse for higher taxes and the abandonment of traditional values. And that's to be expected. Because if you don't have any fresh ideas, then you use stale tactics to scare the voters. If you don't have a record to run on, then you paint your opponent as someone people should run from.

You make a big election about small things.

And you know what – it's worked before. Because it feeds into the cynicism we all have about government. When Washington doesn't work, all its promises seem empty. If your hopes have been dashed again and again, then it's best to stop hoping, and settle for what you already know.

I get it. I realise that I am not the likeliest candidate for this office. I don't fit the typical pedigree, and I haven't spent my career in the halls of Washington.

But I stand before you tonight because all across America something is stirring. What the nay-sayers don't understand is that this election has never been about me. It's been about you.

For 18 long months, you have stood up, one by one, and said enough to the politics of the past. You understand that, in this election, the greatest risk we can take is to try the same old politics with the same old players and expect a different result. You have shown what history teaches us – that, at defining moments like this one, the change we need doesn't come from Washington. Change comes to Washington. Change happens because the American people demand it – because they rise up and insist on new ideas and new leadership, a new politics for a new time.

America, this is one of those moments.

I believe that, as hard as it will be, the change we need is coming. Because I've seen it. Because I've lived it. I've seen it in Illinois, when we provided healthcare to more children and moved more families from welfare to work. I've seen it in Washington, when we worked across party lines to open up government and hold lobbyists more accountable, to give better care for our veterans and keep nuclear weapons out of terrorist hands.

And I've seen it in this campaign. In the young people who voted for the first time, and in those who got involved again after a very long time. In the Republicans who never thought they'd pick up a Democratic ballot, but did. I've seen it in the workers who would rather cut their hours back a day than see their friends lose their jobs, in the soldiers who re-enlist after losing a limb, in the good neighbours who take a stranger in when a hurricane strikes and the floodwaters rise.

This country of ours has more wealth than any nation, but that's not what makes us rich. We have the most powerful military on Earth, but that's not what makes us strong. Our universities and our culture are the envy of the world, but that's not what keeps the world coming to our shores.

Instead, it is that American spirit – that American promise – that pushes us forward even when the path is uncertain; that binds us together in spite of our differences; that makes us fix our eye not on what is seen, but what is unseen, that better place around the bend.

That promise is our greatest inheritance. It's a promise I make to my daughters when I tuck them in at night, and a promise that you make to yours – a promise that has led immigrants to cross oceans and pioneers to travel west; a promise that led workers to picket lines, and women to reach for the ballot.

And it is that promise that, 45 years ago today, brought Americans from every corner of this land to stand together on a Mall in Washington, before Lincoln's Memorial, and hear a young preacher from Georgia speak of his dream.

The men and women who gathered there could've heard many things. They could've heard words of anger and discord. They could've been told to succumb to the fear and frustration of so many dreams deferred.

But what the people heard instead – people of every creed and colour, from every walk of life – is that, in America, our destiny is inextricably linked. That, together, our dreams can be one.

'We cannot walk alone,' the preacher cried. 'And as we walk, we must make the pledge that we shall always march ahead. We cannot turn back.'

America, we cannot turn back. Not with so much work to be done. Not with so many children to educate, and so many veterans to care for. Not with an economy to fix and cities to rebuild and farms to save. Not with so many families to protect and so many lives to mend. America, we cannot turn back. We cannot walk alone. At this moment, in this election, we must pledge once more to march into the future. Let us keep that promise – that American promise – and in the words of Scripture hold firmly, without wavering, to the hope that we confess.

Thank you, and God Bless the United States of America.

Inauguration Address – 20 January 2009

My fellow citizens. I stand here today humbled by the task before us, grateful for the trust you have bestowed, mindful of the sacrifices borne by our ancestors. I thank President Bush for his service to our nation, as well as the generosity and cooperation he has shown throughout this transition.

Forty-four Americans have now taken the presidential oath. The words have been spoken during rising tides of prosperity and the still waters of peace. Yet, every so often the oath is taken amidst gathering clouds and raging storms. At these moments, America has carried on not simply because of the skill or vision of those in high office, but because we the people have remained faithful to the ideals of our forbearers, and true to our founding documents.

So it has been. So it must be with this generation of Americans.

That we are in the midst of crisis is now well understood. Our nation is at war, against a far-reaching network of violence and hatred. Our economy is badly weakened, a consequence of greed and irresponsibility on the part of some, but also our collective failure to make hard choices and prepare the nation for a new age. Homes have been lost; jobs shed; businesses shuttered. Our healthcare is too costly; our schools fail too many; and each day brings further evidence that the ways we use energy strengthen our adversaries and threaten our planet.

These are the indicators of crisis, subject to data and statistics. Less measurable but no less profound is a sapping of confidence across our land — a nagging fear that America's decline is inevitable, and that the next generation must lower its sights.

Today I say to you that the challenges we face are real. They are serious and they are many. They will not be met easily or in a short span of time. But know this, America — they will be met.

On this day, we gather because we have chosen hope over fear, unity of purpose over conflict and discord.

On this day, we come to proclaim an end to the petty grievances and false promises, the recriminations and worn-out dogmas, that for far too long have strangled our politics.

We remain a young nation, but in the words of Scripture, the time has come to set aside childish things. The time has come to reaffirm our enduring spirit; to choose our better history; to carry forward that precious gift, that noble idea, passed on from generation to generation: the

God-given promise that all are equal, all are free, and all deserve a chance to pursue their full measure of happiness.

In reaffirming the greatness of our nation, we understand that greatness is never a given. It must be earned. Our journey has never been one of short-cuts or settling for less. It has not been the path for the faint-hearted — for those who prefer leisure over work, or seek only the pleasures of riches and fame. Rather, it has been the risk-takers, the doers, the makers of things — some celebrated but more often men and women obscure in their labour, who have carried us up the long, rugged path towards prosperity and freedom.

For us, they packed up their few worldly possessions and travelled across oceans in search of a new life.

For us, they toiled in sweatshops and settled the West; endured the lash of the whip and ploughed the hard earth.

For us, they fought and died, in places like Concord and Gettysburg; Normandy and Khe Sahn.

Time and again these men and women struggled and sacrificed and worked till their hands were raw so that we might live a better life. They saw America as bigger than the sum of our individual ambitions; greater than all the differences of birth or wealth or faction.

This is the journey we continue today. We remain the most prosperous, powerful nation on Earth. Our workers are no less productive than when this crisis began. Our minds are no less inventive, our goods and services no less needed than they were last week or last month or last year. Our capacity remains undiminished. But our time of standing pat, of protecting narrow interests and putting off unpleasant decisions – that time has surely passed. Starting today, we must pick ourselves up, dust ourselves off, and begin again the work of remaking America.

For everywhere we look, there is work to be done. The state of the economy calls for action, bold and swift, and we will act – not only to create new jobs, but to lay a new foundation for growth. We will build the roads and bridges, the electric grids and digital lines that feed our commerce and bind us together. We will restore science to its rightful place, and wield technology's wonders to raise healthcare's quality and lower its cost. We will harness the sun and the winds and the soil to fuel our cars and run our factories. And we will transform our schools and colleges and universities to meet the demands of a new age. All this we can do. And all this we will do.

Now, there are some who question the scale of our ambitions – who suggest that our system cannot tolerate too many big plans. Their memories are short. For they have forgotten what this country has already done; what free men and women can achieve when imagination is joined to common purpose, and necessity to courage.

What the cynics fail to understand is that the ground has shifted beneath them – that the stale political arguments that have consumed us for so long no longer apply. The question we ask today is not whether our government is too big or too small, but whether it works – whether it helps families find jobs at a decent wage, care they can afford, a retirement that is dignified. Where the answer is yes, we intend to move forward. Where the answer is no, programmes will end. And those of us who manage the public's dollars will be held to account – to spend wisely, reform bad habits, and do our business in the light of day – because only then can we restore the vital trust between a people and their government.

Nor is the question before us whether the market is a force for good or ill. Its power to generate wealth and expand freedom is unmatched, but this crisis has reminded us that, without a watchful eye, the market can spin out of control – and that a nation cannot prosper long when it favours only the prosperous. The success of our economy has always depended not just on the size of our Gross Domestic Product, but on the reach of our prosperity; on the ability to extend opportunity to every willing heart — not out of charity, but because it is the surest route to our common good.

As for our common defence, we reject as false the choice between our safety and our ideals. Our Founding Fathers, faced with perils we can scarcely imagine, drafted a charter to assure the rule of law and the rights of man, a charter expanded by the blood of generations. Those ideals still light the world, and we will not give them up for expedience's sake. And so to all other peoples and governments who are watching today, from the grandest capitals to the small village where my father was born: know that America is a friend of each nation and every man, woman, and child who seeks a future of peace and dignity, and we are ready to lead once more.

Recall that earlier generations faced down fascism and communism not just with missiles and tanks, but with the sturdy alliances and enduring convictions. They understood that our power alone cannot protect us, nor does it entitle us to do as we please. Instead, they knew that our power grows through its prudent use; our security emanates from the justness of our cause, the force of our example, the tempering qualities of humility and restraint.

We are the keepers of this legacy. Guided by these principles once more, we can meet those new threats that demand even greater effort — even greater cooperation and understanding between nations. We will begin to responsibly leave Iraq to its people, and forge a hard-earned peace in Afghanistan. With old friends and former foes, we'll work tirelessly to lessen the nuclear threat, and roll back the spectre of a warming planet. We will not apologise for our way of life, nor will we waver in its defence, and for those who seek to advance their aims by inducing terror and slaughtering innocents, we say to you now that our spirit is stronger and cannot be broken: you cannot outlast us, and we will defeat you.

For we know that our patchwork heritage is a strength, not a weakness. We are a nation of Christians and Muslims, Jews and Hindus — and non-believers. We are shaped by every language and culture, drawn from every end of this Earth; and because we have tasted the bitter swill of civil war and segregation, and emerged from that dark chapter stronger and more united, we cannot help but believe that the old hatreds shall someday pass; that the lines of tribe shall soon dissolve; that, as

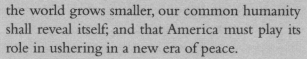

the world grows smaller, our common humanity shall reveal itself; and that America must play its role in ushering in a new era of peace.

To the Muslim world, we seek a new way forward, based on mutual interest and mutual respect. To those leaders around the globe who seek to sow conflict, or blame their society's ills on the West – know that your people will judge you on what you can build, not what you destroy. To those who cling to power through corruption and deceit and the silencing of dissent, know that you are on the wrong side of history; but that we will extend a hand if you are willing to unclench your fist.

To the people of poor nations, we pledge to work alongside you to make your farms flourish and let clean waters flow; to nourish starved bodies and feed hungry minds. And to those nations like ours that enjoy relative plenty, we say we can no longer afford indifference to the suffering outside our borders; nor can we consume the world's resources without regard to effect. For the world has changed, and we must change with it.

As we consider the road that unfolds before us, we remember with humble gratitude those brave Americans who, at this very hour, patrol far-off deserts and distant mountains. They have something to tell us, just as the fallen heroes who lie in Arlington whisper through the ages. We honour them not only because they are guardians of our liberty, but because they embody the spirit of service; a willingness to find meaning in something greater than themselves. And yet, at this moment – a moment that will define a generation – it is precisely this spirit that must inhabit us all.

For as much as government can do and must do, it is ultimately the faith and determination of the American people upon which this nation relies. It is the kindness to take in a stranger when the levees break, the selflessness of workers who would rather cut their hours than see a friend lose their job which sees us through our darkest hours. It is the firefighter's courage to storm a stairway filled with smoke, but also a parent's willingness to nurture a child, that finally decides our fate.

Our challenges may be new. The instruments with which we meet them may be new. But those values upon which our success depends – honesty and hard work, courage and fair play, tolerance and curiosity, loyalty and patriotism – these things are old. These things are true. They have been the quiet force of progress throughout our history. What is demanded then is a return to these truths. What is required of us now is a new era of responsibility – a recognition, on the part of every

American, that we have duties to ourselves, our nation, and the world, duties that we do not grudgingly accept but rather seize gladly, firm in the knowledge that there is nothing so satisfying to the spirit, so defining of our character, than giving our all to a difficult task.

This is the price and the promise of citizenship.

This is the source of our confidence – the knowledge that God calls on us to shape an uncertain destiny.

This is the meaning of our liberty and our creed – why men and women and children of every race and every faith can join in celebration across this magnificent mall, and why a man whose father less than 60 years ago might not have been served at a local restaurant can now stand before you to take a most sacred oath.

So let us mark this day with remembrance, of who we are and how far we have travelled. In the year of America's birth, in the coldest of months, a small band of patriots huddled by dying campfires on the shores of an icy river. The capital was abandoned. The enemy was advancing. The snow was stained with blood. At a moment when the outcome of our revolution was most in doubt, the father of our nation ordered these words be read to the people:

'Let it be told to the future world … that in the depth of winter, when nothing but hope and virtue could survive … that the city and the country, alarmed at one common danger, came forth to meet [it].'

America. In the face of our common dangers, in this winter of our hardship, let us remember these timeless words. With hope and virtue, let us brave once more the icy currents, and endure what storms may come. Let it be said by our children's children that when we were tested we refused to let this journey end, that we did not turn back nor did we falter; and, with eyes fixed on the horizon and God's grace upon us, we carried forth that great gift of freedom and delivered it safely to future generations.

Thank you. God bless you and God bless the United States of America